California Steelhead

CALIFORNIA
STEELHEAD

JIM FREEMAN

The Complete Guide to
Steelhead Fishing in California

Chronicle Books
San Francisco

Library of Congress Cataloging in
Publication Data
Freeman, Jim.
   California steelhead.

   Includes index.
   1. Steelhead fishing—California.
I. Title.   SH687.7.F74 1984
799.1'755   84-11373
ISBN 0-87701-268-7

Editing: Deborah Stone
Composition: Type by Design
Cover photographs: R. Valentine
Atkinson

Chronicle Books
275 Fifth Street
San Francisco, CA 94103

10 9 8 7 6 5 4 3

Contents

California Steelhead

Introduction

Salmon and steelhead fishing is the finest sport for the western fisherman. It presents a great challenge; the angler who masters this game enjoys the sweetest success fishing has to offer. The problems faced by the salmon and steelhead angler are greater than those for most species of migratory fish. This is what makes salmon and steelheading so exciting.

The streams included in this book, rivers ranging from Monterey Bay on the south to the Oregon border at the Smith River and including rivers in the Central Valley, are the best of California streams. Many of these streams are considered comparatively small waters during the summer and early fall months. When winter rains begin, they swell in size and provide some of the finest salmon and steelhead angling to be found in the west.

The streams of the north coast are particularly attractive for the salmon and steelhead angler. Even the smallest streams have a large tidal basin at the mouth. These streams vary in length from short tidal streams like the Garcia and Gualala to lengthy rivers like the Eel and Russian which stretch for many miles and which, in the case of the Eel, have major forks and tributaries. The angler will find a variety of fishing situations and conditions in individual rivers and throughout the entire system of rivers.

Salmon and steelhead that run during the winter months are far different from those found during the summer or fall. Winter-run salmon generally weigh about twenty pounds and steelhead weigh eight pounds on up, which gives them enough weight to be a formidable opponent for the angler. Steelhead also feed little or not at all during their winter migration, which makes them difficult to interest in the angler's lures and baits.

I have checked the stomachs of hundreds of winter steelhead and have found very little in them, unlike those taken in the late summer and fall. Winter-run steelies, if they have anything at all in their stomachs, usually have only the smallest trace of food and virtually none once they leave the tidal stretches of rivers. This means the angler is matching wits with fish that really do not want to eat and that are far more interested in spawning. Salmon don't feed at all during their migration; they will hit lures out of instinct or anger.

Duration of Runs

Timing of a salmon and steelhead fishing trip is all important. It is the key element in success. An old axiom in the fisherman's book is: If there are no fish in the river, you cannot catch them. It is impossible to pin down the element of timing for every stream because the length of time the fish are in any river depends on weather, time of year, and the ripeness of the average salmon and steelhead in a given run.

As a general rule, salmon and steelheads will be running in the northern coastal rivers between mid-November and the end of February, though these runs can begin a few weeks earlier and last almost into the following summer, for steelhead, given the right weather conditions. For the ultimate in winter-run salmon and steelhead success, the angler will need to get the right information along the lengths of the various rivers by using the phone numbers listed in this guide and check the sources supplied here.

The Mattole River is a perfect example of the variation in rainfall that can occur over a very few miles. The Eel River, one of the finest and longest California migratory streams, is located a few miles west of the headwaters of the Mattole, yet the Mattole gets 100 inches of rain per year, according to the records, and the Eel gets perhaps 30 inches each year. This means the Mattole will almost certainly have salmon and steelhead somewhere in its drainage any time after the first serious rainfalls of the season. The amount of rain determines the size of the outflow, which limits the ability of the fish to move through the river system.

The Mattole has the potential of being one of the great salmon and steelhead rivers, but presently it is suffering from an extreme case of overlogging. Until the 1950s, getting logs out of the rugged country in this river drainage was so difficult that the lumber companies went elsewhere. The building boom put a stop to this and the logging companies cut the Mattole and Eel river drainages right down to the rocks. This caused extensive erosion and the very earth washed down into the rivers, stifling successful spawning beds.

In 1983 the Mattole remains one of the most promising prospects for future development. But care must be taken when planning a trip to fish this particular river because it has not yet recovered from the ravages of the logging operations of the past.

The Long and the Short

In order to simplify the treatment of salmon and steelhead fishing in California, the rivers in this guide have been divided into the long and the short streams. Rivers like the Eel, Klamath, Russian, Sacramento, and Smith will be considered long streams. Rivers like the Navarro, Noyo, Gualala, or Garcia will be considered short streams. Some long streams, like Redwood Creek, may drain huge areas but offer fishing only within a few miles of the ocean. Overlogging has caused this situation and has little to do with the stream's potential.

In order to further simplify, if a river, regardless of its length, runs mostly through an area that is closed to the public either by private ownership of the land or by the nature of the land through which it flows, it will be included in the short stream category. The physical length of the stream can be of importance to the fisherman because it takes fish a certain amount of time to proceed upstream into the spawning areas they area seeking. Thus, a long river will almost certainly have fish in it after the first heavy rainfalls, even if scouting the area means traveling a great distance. The important thing is that there are fish to be fished over, the primary goal of the salmon and steelhead fisherman.

The Great Streams

Any of the California salmon and steelhead streams can become great streams to the individual an-

gler. There are a number of factors involved in this. First, the river or creek must have salmon and steelhead in it. This would seem to be the only logical thing to consider. Yet, thousands of fishermen head to the various rivers and creeks along the coast and in the valley of the central part of the state without ever considering if there is even the remotest chance of finding salmon and steelhead. The fact that it is winter, or whatever season it happens to be, does not necessarily mean there will be fish to work over. Sections of this guide will provide information for the reader to call ahead to streamside reporters who can describe fishing conditions on a day-to-day basis.

Certain streams, such as the Klamath, Eel, Smith, Russian, and Sacramento rivers, all qualify for the title of great streams. Some of the elements that determine a great stream are: the volume of water that flows through it, the amount of lumbering or farming that has damaged fishing conditions, the area along the river bank that permits access to the fish, and the physical conditions found during fishing. Every great river has its charms. Every one has its drawbacks.

Generally, the great streams will have some fish most of the year. However, successful fishing will vary with the season. Just like the lesser streams, the great rivers will have definite periods when fishing is good to excellent. In fact, fishing can change from good to poor in a matter of days, depending on a lot of factors, but controlled mostly by the weather.

Rivers like the Klamath start getting a good number of salmon and steelies in July. These early-run fish usually hold in the lower stretches of the river and congregate near the mouths of cooler, tributary streams. In July and August the Klamath can have very warm water. A river like the Trinity, which is a tributary to the Klamath, will also start getting salmon and steelhead in July or August of the average year. Good fishing in both of these rivers usually doesn't start until nearly September. It generally improves into October and through November most years and stays good until heavy rains make fishing conditions difficult.

The Eel, Smith, and Russian rivers, included in the classification of great salmon and steelhead rivers, are more likely to have good fishing in the months between October and February. These are all rivers with modest flows, when compared with rivers like the Klamath or Sacramento, which carry an extremely heavy load of water. But these three rivers are definitely excellent fishing places for the angler who learns how and when to fish them.

The Lesser Streams

A river designated as a lesser stream in this guide does not indicate a lower quality of fishing. Probably the most memorable trips a California salmon and steelhead angler will ever make will take place on these smaller waters. This is what happened to me on a trip in 1959 to the Mattole River. I fished it for a week in early November and hooked and released over 100 steelhead, the smallest of which was over eight pounds and the largest sixteen pounds. I've also had remarkable trips to the Navarro, Garcia, Gualala, and Big rivers.

These lesser streams are certainly not consistent rivers. Most of them do not even run into the ocean during the dry part of the year because sandbars build up around the mouths and plug the outflow of water. As a general rule, any stream south of the Eel River will be like this. These southern streams start producing after the first heavy rains of the year. They can be marvelous to fish when the conditions are right, but most years they are either feast or famine. Persistent rains often knock the lesser streams out of shape for the entire fishing season. This does not mean the angler should forget about fishing them, but he should do research before planning an expensive trip to any of them.

The Sacramento River

I've saved a special spot for the Sacramento River here. It is the premier river in all of California. It, along with its major tributary streams, the Feather, Yuba, and American, forms the most extensive river fishery in California. Few anglers ever think of these major rivers as a source of salmon and steelhead. Even the Department of Fish and Game never pays these Sacramento Valley rivers much attention when it comes to steelheading. The majority of the action concentrated on these rivers goes to salmon fishing.

Fishing any of these valley rivers does take a good deal of thought and planning. Access is limited and often difficult on all of them because most of the river banks are held in private property. This is particularly true of the Sacramento River, where virtually all of the banks of the river are controlled or owned by farmers or ranchers. The prime section for salmon and steelhead fishing is located in the upper reaches of the Sacramento River from Colusa to Redding. Though relatively few anglers fish this part of the river, it is one of the finest salmon and steelhead rivers in California and probably in the west. Fishing conditions are poor for most of the rest of the length of the stream; the lower river up to about Colusa is a deep, sluggish river that has been used more as a canal than a river. When the fish run—salmon almost every month of the year and steelhead primarily in the fall and winter—the river is very low and difficult for the average angler to fish.

King salmon run just about all year, with spring, summer, winter, and fall runs. The spring and fall runs are the top bets for good salmon action. Steelhead fishing is good enough to warrant a fishing effort in the fall, starting in September and lasting until the first heavy rains put the river out of shape. In the last ten years, steelhead have almost stopped going over the counting station at the Red Bluff Diversion Dam, but salmon continue to make the ascent and are taken in good numbers by fishermen working between Red Bluff and Redding.

Most of the year the Sacramento has enough water to make boating reasonably safe, but during the fall months the flows are cut down so much that knowing where to take a boat and where not to becomes a problem. In the spring and summer, the seasons when irrigation is going on in the valley, the river will carry from 8,000 to 14,000 cubic feet of water per second. This is enough so boating is not too hazardous. But in the fall, starting about September, the flows can be cut back to as little as 2,500 to 2,000 feet per second. The angler who is serious about fishing the river during prime times should make every effort to find out how to navigate the flow safely.

Access

Access to the water is so important that a major portion of this guide has been devoted to the problems associated with getting to the water in order to fish. If access to a section of stream is too difficult, even a high-quality section of stream is nearly worthless to the angler. The problems of access are numerous and complicated by the lay of the land, the quality of roads, the seasons, and the type of fishing to be found in any of the rivers.

The access picture on the rivers included in this guide changes rapidly. In the past few years, roads and access trails traditionally used by fishermen have been closed by the owners of the land through which the rivers flow. Often a jet boat or a regular prop boat is the best means of access on the larger streams. Even this is not always satisfactory.

The perfect example of the problems faced by the angler is found in the upper stretches of the Russian and Eel rivers. These two fine streams are physically located only a few miles apart. Either can provide good fishing, depending on many different factors. But virtually all the roads are paved in the Russian River drainage and hardly any of the roads that offer streamside access on the Eel are paved. This makes fishing the upper Eel River a huge problem after the first heavy storms of the season. In fact, fishermen working the Eel can even become trapped by swampy roads if they are camped near the stream when a big Pacific storm moves onshore.

Rules of the Road

Private property owners along the shores of almost all the California salmon and steelhead streams will limit just about all access. Very few will allow free access to the banks of the streams. There is a good reason for this attitude. Private property has been abused by the public. In some cases, it is a good idea to seek out the land owners to get written permission to use roads and access trails.

The salmon and steelhead fisherman should be aware that the bulk of the land on the coastal and mountain rivers is owned by public agencies like the Bureau of Land Management, the Forest Service, and by large lumber companies. The Bureau of Land Management and Forest Service lands belong to the public and access is not only allowed, but encouraged by access roads, trails, campgrounds, and other amenities. Along the coast, the federal and state park systems also have access points, though these are more limited than those of the other public agencies.

Learning to use the roads on lumber company lands is important. I have talked to many managers of lumbering operations and they all want to allow as much public access as possible. But they have had some bad experiences with the general fishing and camping public. As a result, many of them have placed restrictions on how the public uses their lands. The simplest of these is issuing permits for public use. A prime example is in the redwood country, where most of the people who have access permits are local people. This is not because the lumber companies favor local anglers. Rather, local people understand some of the simple rules of the road. In lumber country, when using logging company roads there will be signs that say Drive Right or Drive Left. They mean exactly that because the extremely heavy lumber trucks *always* drive on the inside of the road. They have to; heavy vehicles can cave in the banks or sides of the roads, especially in the wet seasons. The relatively light fisherman's automobile or pickup truck has to drive on the weaker side of the road. Visiting anglers from the city don't have an instinctive understanding of these important and essential rules of the road, whereas local fishermen, who have grown up with these rules, do know instinctively how to operate their vehicles. I've never been refused a permit as long as I was willing to contact the lumber company office and discuss the problems with the managers. Most of them are fishermen and understand the problems of other fishermen.

Checking Conditions

The salmon and steelhead fisherman has to become a weather expert to be consistently successful throughout the seasons. The salmon fisherman is much less concerned with weather and its effects on fishing conditions than is the steelheader. The majority of salmon that run into California waters do so during the late summer, spring, or fall, when storms are not such a serious consideration. In some steelhead streams, like the Trinity, Klamath, Sacramento, and Eel, there are good summer or early fall runs of steelhead and salmon that are not usually hampered by extreme weather changes.

The bulk of the steelheading,

A typical scene on a winter morning. The beginner would do well to watch for this sort of line up. Local anglers and those with experience usually know where the fish hold.

however, takes place during the rainiest time of year. A big winter storm can knock fishing out for varying periods of time, ranging from a week to several weeks, depending on the river. For the purposes of this guide, any storm moving onto the north coast from the Pacific and dropping an inch or more of rain will be considered a major storm. This includes any series of storms where the total rainfall is much over an inch or two. Anything less than this can be considered a small storm.

After a small storm, all the streams in the Mendocino–Sonoma Loop generally take a week to ten days to clear. The exceptions are the Russian and Navarro Rivers, where two weeks is normal. The Eel takes about two weeks to twenty days to clear. Northern streams like the Mad, Van Duzen, the Salmon Rivers, and Redwood Creek will take about a week. The Scott takes two weeks or more. The Smith River clears quickly; a few days is all that is required.

Naturally, these are broad guidelines. The southern streams like the San Lorenzo are in an entirely different type of weather pattern, but generally these streams clear up on the same schedule as the Loop streams.

Conditions also can change rapidly due to lumbering, road building, farm irrigation, and overgrazing by livestock. The serious salmon and steelhead fisherman will take time to find out what effects these have had on his favorite fishing streams.

The time of year and the stage of the season can also make a great deal of difference in the ultimate success of any trip. Very small streams like those in the Sonoma–Mendocino Loop may not get runs of early fish before Christmas, even when there are huge storms that wash out the sandbars at the mouth, thereby providing plenty of water for the moving fish. This also applies to the streams south of the Golden Gate. Both stream systems have had a shortage of water because their flows have been drastically altered in the last hundred years. The bulk of the water that flowed down these smaller rivers has been diverted; the early runs of steelhead and salmon that once ran into every one of them have been eliminated. The only fish that move successfully through these stream systems are those that come in during the winter and spring months. This is unfortunate, but the serious fisherman should take it into consideration before planning a trip.

The steelhead fisherman planning a winter steelhead trip would be well advised to pay a visit to the streams he plans on fishing during their low-water stage in the late fall. By seeing the river at this stage, the angler can determine how to fish when the water rises during the winter. The angler who fishes a great number of streams may want to keep a notebook. It may also be worthwhile for him to get the Geodetic Survey maps of the streams. Some of these are large enough to hold detailed notes of every hold in a long section of river.

Fishing the Loops

When salmon and steelhead fishing, anglers should always be willing to move from one stream to another. Many of the rivers in this guide are physically located only a few miles from one another. A classic example of this is found in the Sonoma–Mendocino Loop streams. This group of rivers includes streams from the Russian River in the south to the Gualala, Garcia, Navarro, and to the north as far as the Tenmile River. It could also include the upper sections of the Eel River and the return loop to the upper sections of the Russian River. These rivers are all considered part of the same loop because they can all be reached in a few hours or minutes of driving time.

Although the Sonoma–Mendocino Loop is the classic example of the California fishing situation, it is by no means the only one. The lower Eel, Mattole, Redwood Creek, Klamath River, and even the Smith River also form a loop that stretches out along the coast. This loop could include many smaller streams like the Van Duzen, which feeds into the lower Eel. The Mad River would be worth checking out for fishermen working any of the rivers along the far north coast.

There are other loops that take some thought. For instance, some loops basically stretch along the length of major rivers. One of these would include the upper Klamath River. Although the Klamath is the most extensive river in this part of the state, it should be considered as only part of the opportunities available to the visiting steelhead and salmon fisherman. While the lower forty miles of the Klamath should be linked to the coast loop of streams, the Klamath from Johnson's and Weitchpec upstream to Iron Gate Dam should be thought of as almost a separate stream. In this loop are the Trinity, Salmon, and

As the tide moves across the bar of the river and into the
coastal streams, it triggers movement of the steelheads. It pays
to keep moving around. Watch for spots where fish are jumping.
This is a good indication of where they will be holding.

Scott Rivers; all major fisheries in their own right. It would be foolish for a visiting angler to fish only the Klamath when there might be good salmon or steelhead action only a few miles away in one of these major tributaries. Many of the larger creeks in this and any other major stream drainage can offer spectacular action if the angler manages to time it right. In fact, moving to the larger creeks and the areas near their mouths can often save a trip if a major storm moves into the area being fished. Often the creeks clear up long before the main river does; salmon and steelhead will crowd into the purer water pouring down the creeks. The angler will find that these fish are much easier to attract than they would be out in the main flows of the river.

The Sacramento River has its own loop. The Feather, Yuba, and American rivers form a loop that will have fish in it at different times. It only takes a few hours to drive to each of these rivers. A boat will be needed to fish these rivers properly; the angler equipped for one river will be equipped for the others. Anglers fishing the Sacramento should be alert to runs on the Feather or the American.

The rule of thumb for fishing any of these loops is that the angler should be ready to move on at a moment's notice to another entirely different stream if the news arrives of a run starting there. Under no circumstances should a salmon and steelhead fisherman pick a single river in any area and stick with it no matter what is happening only a few miles away. This is not the way to be consistently successful when fishing for moving populations of fish. The angler must be willing to move with the migrations.

How Long to Fish

Only experience can tell the angler how long to fish in different situations. If I haven't taken a fish, seen one roll, or received some other indication that I am working over fish, I move on after fifteen to thirty minutes. When I am bait fishing, it takes eight to ten times longer to determine if there are willing fish in a given hold. With a violently whirling or wobbling lure, it takes perhaps a half dozen casts to determine whether the fish are there and willing.

The winter steelheader should never plan to fish a single stream on any given trip. Instead, he should think about winter steelheading from the standpoint of fishing a group of steams. The classic example of this is the Sonoma–Mendocino Loop. In an hour or two of driving time, the angler can reach any one of these rivers from any other in the loop. Fishing can be great in one stream and poor in another just a few miles away. The fisherman should always be ready to move on to another river.

Anglers should be sure to fish in areas where the water is compatible with their equipment. Many times I have seen areas where only fly fishermen were able to take steelies from a given area. Sections of stream that are suitable for both fly and spin fishing at the same time are rare indeed.

Fishing Techniques

Winter-Run Steelhead

Winter steelheading is the greatest challenge for the steelheader. Playing the steelhead game during the winter months takes dedication and skill. The angler who masters winter steelheading enjoys the sweetest success fishing has to offer. The problems faced by the winter steelheader are greater than those taken on by the summer- and fall-run fisherman, but the fish are bigger and more numerous.

The steelhead that runs during the winter months is a different fish from the one in coastal rivers during the summer and fall. Winter-run fish generally average eight pounds or larger, which gives them enough weight to be worthy opponents.

They also feed very little on winter migrations.

I have examined stomach contents of hundreds of steelheads from both winter and summer or fall runs. Very rarely have I ever found an early-run steelie that didn't have food in him. A late-run fish, however, seldom has more than traces of food in his stomach. Thus the angler is matching wits with a fish that really doesn't want to eat and is far more interested in spawning.

How to Catch Steelhead

Fishing a winter-run steelhead stream is far different than fishing for summer- or fall-run fish. In the early runs, steelies will be found in riffles where the oxygen content is high. They also hold just at the point where a riffle breaks off into the depths of a pool or drift. Winter-run steelies are rarely in these jumbled sections of the stream. Instead, they seek spots where the current is smooth and evenly flowing. They seldom will be found in water less than three feet deep and usually are in water from six to ten feet, or a bit deeper. They will sometimes hold in deep, still water, but only when suitable moving water is not available.

It is impossible to be specific about a species like steelheads. One fairly common truth is that steelies seldom will be found in a swirling eddy. I have often taken them from the sides of these big swirls of water but can never remember taking a single one from the center of an eddy. They also do not seem to poke their heads right at the back side of a rock, as would be the case with rainbow trout. They usually hold from a few feet to several feet behind in the slick water formed by the current breaking around the rock. Even then, when I've been in position to see in clear water, the steelies seem to prefer the edges of the slick itself, where the current begins to quicken.

Where brush sweeps the water, and the root system forms deep pockets along the bank, I've seldom found steelies holding right in the hole, near the roots. Instead, they seem to prefer holding at the edge of

Playing a winter fish is an important part of the game. A large winter-run fish should always be beached if possible. Nets and gaffs are seldom used for this kind of fishing, except when using a boat.

Though winter steelies are not noted for their jumping characteristics, some of them put on a good show. In relatively shallow water like this, they haven't got anywhere to go but straight up.

the current and, when the water is clear, darting into the cover of the sweepers.

Many fish are missed by anglers who wade directly into the water when they approach a new section of stream. Remember, there is just as much chance of fish being on your side of the river as on the other. When approaching the water in these small coastal streams, pause for a few moments before actually fishing. I have often taken winter-run steelies by fishing over the top of streamside brush. I have even seen individual fish take an offering.

It is interesting to learn how steelies take a bait. On the Mattole River I have watched fish in clear water as they were taken by bait fishermen working a hole. The fish didn't move up or downstream at all. The only movement they ever made was to fin slowly to one side or another in the current to intercept drifting baits.

If you've ever watched a goldfish feed, you know he doesn't actually move up on a bait. Rather, he opens his mouth to form a suction that draws the food into his mouth. This is what steelies do. The suction effect is fairly strong, too, and light baits can be pulled in from perhaps three or four inches. The bait fishermen missed three times as many hits as they detected: this is a good reason to use yarn over baits to prevent deep hooking of the fish.

Reading the Water

An angler's ability to read water (interpret what the unseen bottom

In big still pools like this, bait, flies, and lures are effective. The riffle at the head of this pool will break into holding water below where the anglers are wading.

structure is like) is the measure of consistent success in steelhead fishing. I can tell an experienced steelheader by watching how he approaches a good drift. In winter fishing in clear water, he will make his first few casts while still well back from the water's edge, and his first few casts will be short.

A rock or obstruction should always be fished. The areas at the tail of a drift, where the water begins to quicken before it heads into the next riffle, is always worth fishing during the winter months. In most riffles there is a V-shaped slick that creases the fast water of the main riffle. Fish move up either side of these slicks. They usually then move to one side of the V and pause to rest. This is particularly true if that section of stream has a lot of riffles or if the riffle is a particularly long or turbulent one.

Submerged boulders can be located by noting burbled water or a slick formed by the action of the water breaking over the boulder surface. This is true of any kind of underwater obstruction.

A very good spot for steelies is where a large boulder breaks up the length of a long riffle. Steelies will usually pause to rest behind any large boulder like this. This is particularly true as the fish get further upstream near the spawning beds. They are more tired and pause for longer periods to rest.

If you take a steelhead from a certain spot, try to remember everything you can about fishing that particular hold. A successful steelheader does very little different from the unsuccessful fisherman, but those small differences are all-important. The lowering of the rod tip can be critical at a certain point in a drift. In fact, if you begin tapping along the bottom and suddenly there is a long pause in the tapping, it's a good idea to fish the spot carefully. Very probably you have located a depression or hole in the bottom. Any steelie in that section will be in the hole to get out of the current.

Even on long stretches of water, where a casual fisherman will see no difference from one part to another, a careful fisherman can see tiny differences in surface currents. A mere curling of the current can mean a lot. The change in surface flow is directly affected by the shape of the bottom and by unseen obstructions.

Always remember where you take a fish. You can probably take another one from this spot if conditions are the same the next time you fish it. In fact, with a dozen good holds the experienced steelheader can usually catch a limit any time there are fish in that section of river.

Where to Catch Steelheads

Although steelies can be found anywhere in the length of a stream, there are certain sections that warrant special attention. I've already mentioned bridges and their nearby areas. Another excellent spot is near the mouth of the stream. In fact, this is such a productive spot

This angler has chosen the proper spot to begin casting to steelheads. They rarely lay or hold in white water.

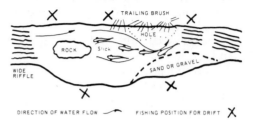

DIRECTION OF WATER FLOW ⟶   FISHING POSITION FOR DRIFT ✕

Note how steelies take advantage of flow change by using rock. They will seldom be found in deep holes or under sweepers of brush trailing in water.

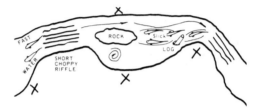

Though steelies use protected flow of rocks or logs, they shy away from fast riffles.

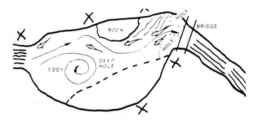

Steelies generally avoid deep holes or bars. They hold at the edges of current flow. Note area above bridge.

Complex currents caused by submerged rocks should always be fished with care. Broken surface is a sign of sunken obstruction. Note special spots where the angler should stand while fishing this situation.

in some streams that it is illegal to fish within a certain radius of the mouth. The Mattole River is like this.

Usually boats are needed to fish the mouth of the stream effectively. But spots like the mouth of the Russian and the Smith are well known for their high-quality shore fishing. The reason these spots are so effective is that steelies, as well as other migratory fish, pause there when they get their first taste of fresh water. After all, they've had a steady diet of pure salt water for most of their lives.

Another spot well worth checking is the upper limit of high tide in any stream. This is an area of constant change, and steelies are noted for their reaction to any change. Places like Minor Hole on the Garcia, Brown's Pool and Austin Riffle on the Russian, and the pools below the Dr. Fine Memorial Bridge on the Smith are all famous as steelhead-producing areas. The same used to be said for Singley Hole on the Eel. Now the action spot is nearer Fernbridge.

The four drawings included with this section are meant as a brief guide to where steelies will probably be found. All streams are made up of a few different types of water. In the drawings, I have attempted to cover most types of river conditions the angler will face. The only situation I have left out is fishing deep holding holes in the tidal basin. Here, I've found that steelies hold along the sides of the deeper holes and usually not in the very center of the deepest parts. This means that the angler should cast into the deepest part of the holes and work lures, baits, or flies back up along the slope. Plunking—casting out and letting a bait lay—is not a successful method for the vast majority of steelhead fishing situations.

Note in the drawing how the bulk of all fish are in the center or drift sections of pools and runs. If there is an obstruction, note that the fish are also strung out in the protection of the rock, log, or other midstream or streamside object. This is particularly true of bridge abutments.

Steelies prefer a bottom made up of rubble rather than sand or gravel. Often, though, when they are unable to find a rubbled or broken bottom, they will be found in a depression in the bottom, if one is available. If even this amenity is absent, steelheads will choose a spot along the bank where there is a measure of protection from the current by the friction of water moving along the bank.

Klamath River Steelhead

The Klamath River is the type of fishing stream that causes writers and anglers to become lyrical. The sight and feel of anadromous fish such as the king salmon, silver salmon, or steelhead in a big brawling stream like the Klamath will cause any serious angler to catch his breath in anticipation and wonder. In the fall and winter months, when there are many runs of these seagoing fish, anglers gather from all over the world to sample the Klamath River drainage—known as one of the finest fishing areas in the world.

Not only is the fishing magnificent in the Klamath river drainage, but the stream and its tributaries move through some of the most primitive and beautiful mountains in all of North America. The angler

A Klamath River steelhead does his stuff for a spin fisherman.

can expect to find excellent sport and take fish in a setting that will give him deep satisfaction. The river has been noted, since Zane Gray made it famous in his writings, as the place to be for steelhead and salmon fishing at its very finest.

Klamath River steelheads are a very special breed of fish, different from steelies found almost anywhere else. The only other stream that has comparable steelheads is the Rogue River in Oregon. Klamath steelheads are a smaller, more streamlined, and harder fighting steelhead than any I've found in streams from California to Alaska.

The average Klamath steelie will be from three to perhaps six pounds. Steelheads over or under that weight are exceptional in this river. In the middle range of four or five pounds, and fresh run during the mild months of late summer and fall, the steelhead seems to reach the very peak of his fighting spirit. At this size he has enough muscle to give a good account of himself when he is hooked. Steelies are so numerous in the Klamath River that the angler can expect to do battle with several in a single trip rather than have to settle for one or two fish, as is the case in most steelhead streams.

The thing that makes Klamath River steelheads stand out is their almost unlimited vitality. Even in the upper reaches of the river during the latter part of the fall, Klamath steelheads jump more often and fight harder and longer than most steelheads found in other streams. It is not uncommon for a fresh fall-run steelhead to make more than a dozen smashing, clean, clear leaps before he even begins to make his stand in the heavy currents of the river and is played to the place where he is beached. I know of no other strain of steelhead that will strip a large steelhead fly or spin reel faster than the Klamath River variety when taken under the proper conditions.

Klamath River steelheads are numerous. The Department of Fish and Game estimates that approximately a quarter of a million of them enter the mouth of the Klamath each year. These fish fan out through the entire Klamath River and into the other streams in the drainage. Since the Department of Fish and Game estimates that only about 30,000 of these steelheads are taken annually, the fishing should last as long as man does not interfere with the runs by building dams or polluting the stream.

When to Take Steelheads

I have often said that only a lunatic would try to predict when a run of steelheads or any anadromous fish would occur in any particular section of a Pacific Coast stream. There are so many variable elements that even the best thought out predictions can go astray by weeks or even by months. A huge storm such as the one that hammered the Klamath River drainage in 1964 can put the runs of migrating fish off their normal schedule for years.

However, to help the visiting angler as much as possible to make an educated guess, I will give a roundup of approximately the best

A typical Klamath steelhead. Taking them with flies offers anglers the ultimate in sport.

This is the reason anglers travel from all over the world to do battle with Klamath steelheads. The long run of water here is ideal for fly fishing.

times to plan a steelheading trip to the Klamath River.

In his fine brochure, "Angling Guide to the Klamath River," Millard Coots wrote for the Department of Fish and Game: "One competent authority has described the general upstream progress by steelheads as follows: Weitchpec (mouth of Trinity River), August 8; Orleans, August 20; Somes Bar (mouth of Salmon River), August 24; Happy Camp, September 7; Scott River, September 20; Shasta River, October 3; and Klamath (below Iron Gate Dam), October 8."

Based on years of fishing the Klamath River myself and from writing about the stream in newspapers and magazines, I have to take my hat off to Millard Coots' "competent authority" and say that I

would choose to be in these same places about two or three weeks later than the timetable. I feel that then the visiting angler would have the best chance of hitting the middle or central part of the steelhead runs in the Klamath River.

My own timetable would be Blue Creek to Johnson's, September 1; Weitchpec, September 7; Orleans to Somes Bar, September 20; Happy Camp, October 1; Happy Camp to Iron Gate Dam, the whole month of October.

I would change the timetable officially produced by the Department of Fish and Game because I found that the steelies rarely move out of the tidal bore area below Blue Creek and the tidal area in the lower level of the river until some upstream influence, such as increased releases from the Iron Gate or Copco Dams in the far upper reaches of the river, causes the fish to become restless.

I also think that the steelheads begin to slow their pell-mell movements up the Klamath as they reach the area above Happy Camp. Here they start to slow down to follow the king salmon runs beginning to move onto the spawning beds; they also start to hang around the mouths of the feeder streams. As soon as a really good rain hits the Klamath drainage, these steelheads will move out of the main river. Then new runs will move into the holding pockets in the upper river.

A very rainy year, or a very dry one, can knock any timetable into a cocked hat when it comes to fishing any steelhead stream. The Klamath is no different. Rains make locating a run of steelies more difficult and also cause the runs to move a lot faster through the main parts of the stream. During an extremely dry year, the steelheads tend to anchor or hold in the deeper and faster flowing sections of the river. This can be good or it can cause the fish to sulk in deep holes where they are virtually impossible to tempt into striking any kind of offering.

For an overall guide to when to be on the Klamath River, it is reasonably certain that steelheads will be on hand in the main part of the river at some given spot any time after the middle of August. Later in

A typical bright Klamath River steelhead will run from about three to five pounds. They are known for fighting ability rather than size. A worthy opponent on any kind of tackle, Klamath River steelheads provide the supreme sport for the fly fisherman.

Soon after the salmon arrive in the summer months, fighting steelheads like these begin to show in the lower Klamath River. These fresh-run steelies are famous for the amount of fight they put up.

the season – through February and the spring months of the following year – they are more scattered through the main river and have spread out into the tributary streams. These late-run steelheads are much larger and not nearly as lively as the summer- and fall-run specimens.

Actually, there are at least a few steelheads in the Klamath River and the feeder streams of the entire river drainage all twelve months of the year. Even during June and July reports of scattered steelhead catches come in. Usually these fish are taken by vacationing anglers fishing for small breeder steelheads and salmon that grow in the streams before migrating to the ocean. These scattered steelheads,

taken during the off-season months, are hardly worth the visiting angler's time. They are usually shy and very difficult to take, even if a stretch where these lay-over steelheads are holding can be located. Only the local anglers who fish the streams in the drainage know where these fish are laying over waiting to spawn during the next season.

Where to Take Steelheads

In general, the closer you are to the headwaters, the less water you will have to deal with when you fish for steelheads in the Klamath River. Near the mouth of the river, any-where below the mouth of Trinity River at Weitchpec, the Klamath is a huge, deep, and fast-moving stream.

The angler who wants to take his fish in the early fall should plan on dealing with this heavy water and on fishing the lower reaches of the stream only in selected spots from shore. Otherwise he must be willing to work from a boat.

The middle sections of the Klamath—from the mouth of the Salmon River at Somes Bar to the mouth of the Trinity River at Hamburg and Scotts Bar—is still a huge stream for the angler working with lighter tackle suited to taking four- to six-pound steelheads. But here you will find the river starting to change markedly in character. It is possible to find plenty of eddies and riffles where the angler who can cast a good fly line or who likes to use light spinning tackle will be able to cover his share of steelheads.

Above the mouth of the Scott River, the Klamath alternatively dives into ravines that are all but complete barriers to fishing access or opens up into beautiful valleys where the angler can find any type of fishing water he could hope for.

When it comes to locating a run of fish in the Klamath River at a specific time, the angler is faced with the job of narrowing down his choice of river sections to an area small enough so that he can fish a reasonable amount of water each day until he manages to score. A visiting angler may zero in on a run of steelies and then find the run holding in a section of stream located in a very steep canyon. In the nearly 200 miles of stream in the main Klamath River alone, there are several stretches that are impossible to

This nice steelhead was caught using the popular flatfish lure.

reach by normal access and that must be fished from a professionally operated float or jet boat.

With the exception of the upper reaches of the river, the Klamath is a large stream that varies from between 100 to 200 feet wide through most of its course. The visiting angler may also locate a run of steelheads in a section of the stream where the river is so big that he has to know the exact kind of equipment to take along to do an effective job.

The character of the Klamath River varies almost from mile to mile along its length. In general, the river drops from between ten feet to eighty feet per stream mile. In the sections where the Klamath drops at the ten feet per mile rate, the angler can expect to find good water for light tackle fishing with spinning, baitcasting, or fly fishing equipment. But in the sections where the river flows over steeply dropping terrain, the angler who tries to fish with very light tackle will be hopelessly undergunned if he tries to use any but the stoutest fishing tackle.

The maps accompanying this guide note the best section of the Klamath for various methods of fishing. Access is the key to success in fishing the Klamath. Tackle and techniques are standard in different sections of the river. These are detailed in conjunction with the maps.

Klamath River Salmon

The king salmon is the major species of Pacific salmon taken in the Klamath River. The big kings use the river and its many tributaries as a spawning ground; their annual migration attracts anglers from all over the world.

The bulk of the king salmon taken in the Klamath by sport anglers are taken in the lower section of the stream. It is here, close to tidewater, that king salmon are at their best. In the month of July during most years, kings begin to make their runs into the tidal basin at the mouth of the river. Most of them do not actually begin their upstream migrations to the spawning beds through the drainage; instead, they begin to run into tidewater and then return to the ocean as the tides rise and fall at the mouth of the river.

These early-run salmon normally come into the tidal basin to feed on the baitfish that are found in the lagoon at the mouth of the river and in the ocean near the mouth. It is this great July action that attracts so many vacationing anglers.

A small number of king salmon can be found somewhere in the drainage and in the main Klamath River nearly every month of the year. The heavy fall runs usually begin sometime during the month of August when groups of king salmon leave the tidewater section of the river and begin moving steadily upstream. In the average year, the heaviest parts of these annual migrations take place through the tidewater area and into the main part of the lower river during September and early October.

As each successive wave or group of salmon enter the river, they are met by more and more anglers until a peak is reached right around the Labor Day weekend. At this time of year, the salmon and a few migrating steelheads will be found in all of the lower river generally, from the sandbar at the mouth of the river upstream as far as the mouth of the Trinity River and Bluff Creek.

The California Department of

The coast near the mouth of the Klamath offers some excellent sightseeing opportunities.

Fish and Game estimates that approximately 168,000 king salmon use the Klamath River and its tributary streams each year for spawning. Of this total it is estimated that approximately 28,000 are taken by anglers fishing in the river and its tributaries. This means that something like 16 percent of the salmon available in the river system are being utilized in the sport take each year — definitely not an excessive amount.

One reason that the lower sections of the Klamath provide so much of the fishing in a normal year is the fact that nearly half, or some 80,000, of the total king salmon that enter the Klamath River migrate up the first major tributary into the Trinity River. While the fall runs are the heaviest of the runs of king salmon into the Klamath River drainage, other smaller runs enter in the spring months, generally to spawn in larger tributaries such as the Trinity, Scott, and Salmon Rivers.

Silver Salmon

The fighting silver salmon also uses the lower Klamath River and its tributaries for spawning. The silvers normally begin to arrive just about the time that the heaviest runs of king salmon begin to taper off, usually from the middle of September through November. The peak of silver salmon action in the lower river takes place in October.

The silvers usually do not run into the headwaters of the Klamath at Iron Gate Dam. The normal upper limit is the Scott River area. Most of the smaller tributaries that feed into the lower Klamath get at least a few silver salmon spawners.

The annual runs of silvers normally number about 15,000 fish and the take of this species is relatively light. Like the king salmon, some silvers are on the move during an extended period of time. When an angler fishing for salmon hooks into a silver, he will know it at once because silvers are far more likely to put on a spectacular aerial display than the generally larger king salmon.

In distinguishing a silver salmon from a king, the two important things to note are the mouth color and the tail markings. A silver salmon has black spots only on the upper lobe of the tail and, unlike the king salmon which generally has a completely black mouth, has a whitish line that runs along the gum line where the teeth will form.

Best Salmon Spots

While steelheads are more likely to be found in the riffles and glides of fast water, salmon are more prone to rest in deeper slower sections of the river. They are also more likely to be found bunched up in the deeper water close to the major tributary streams, including some of the larger creeks in the Klamath River drainage. This does not mean that salmon are never taken in riffles or glides of water. However, usually when they are in this part of the stream, they are migrating and will only occasionally be willing to strike at a lure or bait.

In the tidewater section of the stream, kings and silvers are taken in large numbers by both bank and boat fishermen. The bank fishermen generally use lures or rigged bait-fish and long surf casting rods. Probably the best spot to shore fish is right at the mouth of the river or in the area immediately near the mouth.

At one time, anglers used to form lines of boats and anchor right at the mouth of the river. This was such a dangerous procedure that the Coast Guard now prohibits anchoring in these rows. Instead, anglers troll in waters off the Requa shore and in the main migrational channel on the north side of the big islands just upstream from the mouth. A few anglers merely troll at random with lures and rigged baits, but the majority of successful fishermen in the tidal basin stay close to the deeper channels.

In the upstream section of the river, kings and salmon will hit fairly well even though they do not do any sort of feeding once they begin their migrations toward the spawning beds. The best spots through the years to take salmon have been near the mouths of Blue Creek, Trinity River, Bluff Creek, Salmon River, Indian Creek, Scott River, Horse Creek, Beaver Creek, Shasta River, and the final few miles of river before reaching the Iron Gate Fish Ladder. An angler who fished only these spots would probably end up each season with as many or more salmon as anglers who fished many different areas of the 200-mile-long river.

It is always a good idea to stop at local tackle shops and ask where the salmon are hitting. There can be small areas of stream that are crammed with salmon and then there can be stretches of several miles that are unproductive, even if salmon are on hand or are moving through the area. Areas where fish will hit an angler's offering change slightly from year to year. Generally, however, the river returns to its same form and salmon can usually be found in the same areas year after year.

How to Catch Salmon

In general, it can be said that the deeper in the Klamath River the angler fishes, the more chance he has to go home with a limit of salmon. Very rarely will a salmon rise very far off the bottom of the stream to take a lure or bait. An exception to this may be the case of very fresh-run silver salmon that enter the Klamath each fall. Silvers will occasionally take lures and baits, including large streamer flies at or near the surface. Soon after the silvers leave the tidewater section of the stream, they lose interest in chasing their food.

Whether the angler is fishing right near the mouth of the stream or over 200 miles upstream near the Iron Gate Hatchery and Fish Ladder, the best method of taking these salmon is to fish as deeply as possible without actually snagging lure, fly, or bait on the bottom. In the vast majority of cases, this also applies to steelhead fishing. Steelies will occasionally rise for a fly or lure, but for every one that will come up off the bottom to take a surface offering, a thousand others will hit deep in the current, at or near the bottom of the stream.

Most of the tackle that works well for Klamath River salmon and steelhead is gear that allows the angler to control the depth at which he is fishing. This depth control is very touchy because of the vagaries of the current and tide in each area of the stream. Add to this the various weights and sizes of lures, baits, and flies and you have an endless variety of situations. There are certain basic rigs that have been worked out over the years by Klamath River regulars, however, that will help the newcomer fish this big stream.

To a great extent, the gear used for Klamath River salmon fishing is very much like that used for steelhead fishing. In some cases the main difference is only in the strength of the tackle used for the two different species. An average Klamath River king salmon will range anywhere from a couple of pounds up to thirty pounds. Obviously, the tackle used for a five-pound steelie is not suitable for taking big, fresh-run king salmon or the bigger silver salmon.

As in any compromise, something must be given in each case so the angler does not wind up with tackle that is too light for one species and too heavy for the others. In many cases all three species – silver, king salmon, and steelheads – are active at the same time in the same general areas. All three species will often hit the same lures and baits, so the selection of tackle for general fishing should be given particular attention, depending on what part of the stream the angler will be fishing.

Ocean Salmon

Probably the easiest way to get into California salmon fishing is to fish in the ocean. The ocean sport catch of salmon, both king and coho (or silver) salmon, is much larger than the stream sport catch. California has several sport fishing ports along the coast from Monterey to the Oregon border. The major ports, where ocean fishermen can either hire a party boat or launch a private boat for ocean fishing, are San Francisco and Monterey in the central coastal area; and Fort Bragg, Eureka, and Crescent City along the north coast. Other ports such as Half Moon Bay, Bodega Bay, Shelter Cove, and Trinidad have launch facilities for private boats and party-boat operations, though most of the fishing done from these ports is for other species. As a general rule, more king salmon are taken in the central coast areas, especially out of the Golden Gate at San Francisco. Anglers who want a good chance of taking both species of salmon would do better choosing one of the northern ports. The total take and the number of fisherman-days of angling per year are estimated by the California Department of Fish and Game for these major ports. The angler can get a fair idea of how successful he will be by checking these statistics.

In the most recent year for which there are statistics, San Francisco anglers spent 101,300 days of angling and took 114,600 king salmon and 2,000 silver salmon for an average of better than one fish per rod for each fishing trip. In the preceding years, between 1979 a 1981, an average of 95,466 anglers took an average of 82,566 king salmon and an average of 666 silvers for a rod-average of less than one fish per rod. The 1982 season was one of the best in a decade.

At three north coast ports, Crescent City, Eureka, and Fort Bragg, the total number of king salmon taken in the 1982 season was 20,900 and the total coho take was 22,500 for a total of 43,400 fish. These fish were taken with 53,800 angler-days of effort for well under a fish per rod average. However, if the angler wants to do battle with the scrappy, but smaller coho, this would be the choice area to fish. Again, the 1982 season was one of the best in many years. A rundown of the catch-success ratio for the four major California ports for the four years between 1979 and 1982 shows that San Francisco anglers got 1.06 fish per angler-day of effort; Fort Bragg was .77 per rod; Eureka was .65 per rod; Crescent City was .53 salmon of both types per rod. However, Eureka had, by far, the best per-rod average for silver salmon on the entire California coast. These figures show that as the angler works further to the north he can expect a smaller average per rod take today.

Partyboat Fishing

Partyboat fishing is probably the surest way to become familiar with ocean salmon fishing along the California coast. A partyboat is just what its name suggests: a commercial, licensed boat of larger size that is used to take several fishermen out onto the ocean to fish for a day or part of a day. The party can consist of several fishermen who all know each other or it can be made up of anglers from several different areas, all booked on an open basis. Frequently, the bookings are arranged by a bait and tackle store, through a central booking agent working for an individual, or through a group of party boat owners and skippers. The idea is to keep the cost to each individual fisherman down enough so that people from all walks of life can afford to go for a day of salmon trolling on the ocean. A party trip could number from a dozen to two dozen anglers. Because the lines are all being trolled at the same time, the type of equipment used for this kind of fishing is determined more by the conditions than by the salmon.

For the first few trips on a party-boat, a newcomer to ocean salmon trolling would probably be wise to use the tackle for rent by the party-boat operator. These rigs, suited for handling the largest salmon under the most difficult possible situations, are available for a few dollars. All the terminal tackle and the necessary cannonball weights are also available on board the party-boat. The word *cannonball* almost exactly describes the heavy, three-pound iron weights used for trolling on board party boats when many fishermen are fishing at the same time. An individualistic angler cannot use equipment much different from what is being used by the rest of the fishermen. If one or two anglers use lighter or heavier weights than those prescribed by the partyboat skipper, the lines would trail out at different angles than the lines of the rest of the fishermen. Terrible snagging and turmoil would result. The skipper can also determine where the salmon and the baitfish are under the boat by watching the electronic equipment and can instruct fishermen using approximately the same equipment how far to let their lines down to keep baits and lures in the schools of salmon. The stout rods, heavy lines, and heavy reels are used to control and operate the raising and lowering of the three-pound ball trolling weights rather than to fight and defeat salmon once it is finally hooked. An angler wanting to experiment with lighter tackle must find a skipper who is also willing to experiment.

The cannonball is rigged with a special sinker-releasing device. When a salmon hits, a spring release mechanism is tripped and the ball sinker drops to the bottom, leaving the fisherman to handle the salmon on an unencumbered line. Even then, on a partyboat, an angler is expected to pressure the fish into the net as soon as possible, since all the fishermen aboard have to wait until each individual salmon is netted. If two or more salmon are hooked at the same time, as when the trolls are made through a large school of willing salmon, the individual angler is expected to control his fish to keep from tangling his line with other anglers. There is always a deckhand aboard a party-boat to advise those anglers who have hooked fish and to tell anglers who haven't yet hooked fish to bring in their line so that the anglers with hookups can play their fish up to the net.

Most anglers who decide to buy their own fishing equipment for ocean trolling end up with a very stout rod and with line that tests about thirty pounds. If they do most of their fishing from a partyboat, they usually choose rods about 5½ to 6 feet long. If they fish from a private boat, they usually use rods of 7 or 7½ feet. The reason for the extra length on a private boat is that it gives a better feel of the fighting fish. Private boats are never as crowded as partyboats. The shorter rod is preferred on a crowded partyboat. The angler working from a private boat may slim his line down to about 20-pound test and use smaller weights to get down to the proper depths.

In ocean trolling, it doesn't matter whether an angler chooses spinning or level wind reels, although the vast majority of serious ocean salmon fishermen use star drag, level wind saltwater reels. There is little if any casting done in most areas where king salmon are found. However, off the north coast the coho and king salmon will often be close enough to the surface so that lighter tackle, perhaps a 9-foot spinning rod with 15-pound test line should be kept rigged and ready to use. Often the salmon will start feeding on bait, driving it to the surface where they can be taken by casting into the seething schools of baitfish. A boat that repeatedly trolled through these bait schools would certainly put them down to the depths. Partyboat skippers rarely allow anglers to cast into feeding schools. It could be very dangerous for a couple dozen anglers of differing talents to cast in the hectic atmosphere of a school of salmon in a feeding frenzy.

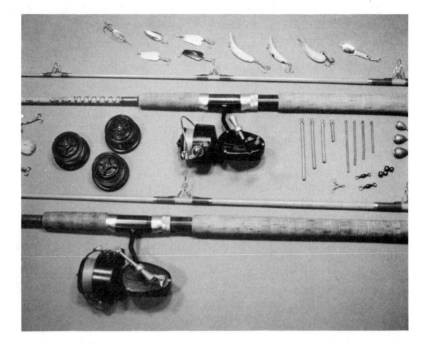

Equipment

Winter Steelhead

Fishing the north coast streams during the winter months takes more equipment than fishing almost any other sort of stream system. The reason for this is that the streams range from small brooks in the upper stretches to very large bays in the tidal sections. The winter steelheader can rarely afford to be a specialist in his tackle selection if he wants to be consistently successful. The situation will dictate the type of equipment used in almost every case.

I have been trying to simplify my own rod and reel selections for many years. Although I've managed to lop off several rigs from my own arsenal, I am still stuck with carrying more rods and reels along on each trip than I'd like to.

Choosing a First Rig

If the angler is new to steelhead fishing and doesn't own any equipment specifically designed for the sport, he can put together a rig that will cover most situations. The rod should be 9 feet in length and the action should be about the same as found in the Fenwick FS 90. The reel should be of good quality equal to that found in the Mitchell 300. Most important is to have a few extra spools filled with the right size lines.

The great advantage to spin fishing reels is that it is easy to change line sizes to meet changing stream conditions. All good reels have this feature. The steelhead is a powerful fish by any measurement and fresh line should always be used. You don't have to buy expensive lines as long as you change them every couple of trips.

If the angler has spools fitted with 10-, 8-, and 12-, 15-, and 6-pound test lines he can be certain he is ready for any situation he could possibly face on coastal streams. The lines are listed here in the order of importance. The angler should at least have spools fitted with 10-, 8-, and 12-pound test. These should be loaded to the proper place on the reel, within one-eighth inch of the edge of the spool.

If the angler already has an outfit built around a rod of 6½ to 8 feet, no new outfit is needed. The shorter rods will allow you to fish the majority of situations faced on all the coastal streams. As long as the angler beefs up his line to deal with a strong fish like the steelie, he can get action with a shorter rod.

All-Purpose Rigs

Of all the rods and reels I use, my Fenwick FS 70 probably gets more service on winter steelhead streams than any other. This rod, fitted with a Mitchell 300 reel and the proper line size for the situation I am fac-

A good selection of spoons and spinners is essential in steelhead fishing. Your selection should include a variety of sizes as shown here.

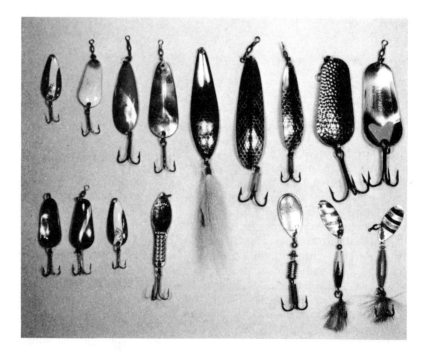

ing, does a good job in most cases. The rod is surprisingly powerful for such an easy-to-use size. It will handle a good range of weights, which is an important item.

I also use a Fenwick FS 90 a great deal when I am fishing the lower stretches of the coastal streams. This rod can be fitted either with a light saltwater reel or, as I prefer, with an Ambassadeur 6000 reel for maximum distance casting. I put 12- pound test monofilament on this reel and can handle enough distance to cover most pools in the tidal basins.

The problem with selecting a steelhead rig is that the rod, reel, and line have to be combined in such a way that the steelheader can get a maximum of distance and sensitivity. It would do little good to boom out a long cast if the angler had to use weights of much more than a few ounces. A heavy weight nails the lure or bait to the bottom; drift fishing is almost impossible with any measure of rod tip sensitivity.

The winter-run steelie is a notoriously soft-mouthed feeder. They merely stop a drifting bait or lure, in most cases, and the only indication the angler gets is a slight pause in the drift of the bait. With a stiff-tipped rod, it is hard to tell the difference between a soft strike and the gentle nodding of the rod tip as the bait, lure, and weight drift slowly along in the current.

Specialized Rigs

I use what is called a meat rod, made from a 10-foot Harnell 675R rod fitted with oversize spinning guides and an Ambassadeur 6000 reel with 12-pound test monofilament. This is a rugged outfit to use

for fishing long periods of time. My arms begin to feel like lead after a few hours of holding this rig up at an angle. However, I can reach out there to probe a lure or bait through almost any hole that can't be reached with lesser tackle. Also, a two- or three-ounce terminal rig will put a fair bend into this rod to give reasonable distance and the necessary delicacy needed for good winter fishing. This rig, though, is a beast to use where there is very much streamside brush. It's a rig I use only for specialized situations.

Winter Fly Fishing

Many anglers feel fly fishing is a poor way to take winter-run steelheads. This is not correct. When the right conditions exist for fly fishing, where the water is clear enough so a steelhead can see a fly, this can be the best way to take fish. Some years there are long periods when there is little or no rainfall. The water in coastal streams clears up; this is when fly fishing is the deadliest way to take steelies.

The rig I've used more than any other is a Fenwick FF 108 fitted with the proper size line of around 300 grains. I prefer fast-sinking lines for winter fishing because winter-run steelheads are always found right on the bottom. The Fenwick FF 95 is also a good selection for this kind of fishing. In any case, the use of shooting heads or shooting tapers is now almost universal in coastal stream fishing.

A shooting head is the first thirty feet of a tapered line cut off and a loop of line added to the back, heavy end. These shooting tapers are used to get casts of good distance, up to and over 100 feet. With the rods mentioned above, a good caster should be able to get casts of around 100 feet on dry ground and perhaps 80 feet when wading to hip depths. If the proper line is fitted on these rods and you are not getting these distances, it is the fault of the caster and not the rig.

Winter Flies

There is a good deal of truth to the statement by the late Bill Bucknam of Bigfoot Lodge, when asked which of the thousands of patterns to use for fishing the Klamath River, "Just pick a fly and go find a steelhead." A steelie is, after all, a visitor in the stream rather than a tenant. In winter they feed little, if at all, on their spawning migration.

In the lower sections of any stream, brighter patterns such as Fall Favorite or shrimp patterns seem to produce best. As fish move into the upper stretches of the same streams, they develop the same tastes as native trout and feed more readily on darker patterns such as the Silver Hilton and nymph patterns. This seems logical. When they are closer to the ocean, they probably remember saltwater feed such as small fishes and shrimps. As they move upstream, they probably forget these items and, if they feed at all, must take the underwater food found in the streams.

I think size is the only real difference between one pattern and another. I have often seen several anglers take fish from a pool, such as Brown's Pool on the Russian, on the same day. The patterns were different but the successful fisher-

Spinning gear can be used for fishing in any of the stream areas and lakes featured in this guide. It is the easiest and most versatile type of equipment to use.

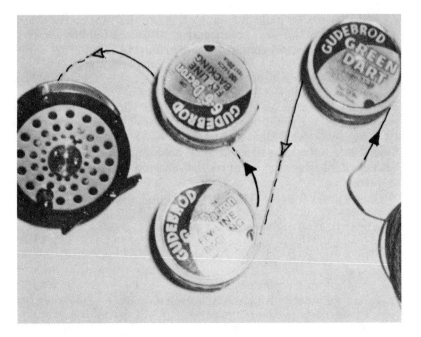

The proper way to rig a shooting head or shooting taper fly line for Klamath River fishing: Tie limp monofilament line to fly line at right, using only one hundred feet of mono. Tie monofilament to dacron fly line backing to fill spool of large fly reel at left.

men almost always had flies of the same size.

Flies for winter-run steelies should be as heavy as required to get them down to the bottom but there is a definite limit to how heavy the fly should be. The first time you rap yourself in the ear on a frosty winter morning you'll know you've reached the practical limit of fly weight. There are only three ways to properly weight a fly: add weight *in* the hook, add weight *to* the hook, or add weight to the leader just in front of the fly. Of these three I prefer to add weight in the hook. Heavy wire hooks are available for this.

Wrapping fuse lead wire around the hook shank before tying on the body is next best. Adding bead chain eyes is another way to add weight, in patterns such as the Boss. This can be used with any fly pattern with no damage to the pattern. Least effective is to add split shot to the leader. If you must add weight to the leader, clip the shot on right at the knot on the fly. This avoids the unpleasant pendulum effect of a shot placed some distance up the line. I don't believe it has any bad effect on the action or effectiveness of the fly.

Yarn Fly

A specialized fly, the Yarn Fly, can be used very effectively by spin fishermen to take winter-run steelheads. The yarn fly is tied with wool, normally fluorescent yarn. Some anglers prefer treble hooks, but single hooks of adequate size catch and hold fish much better than trebles.

The fly is made by tying a dozen or more two-inch pieces of yarn at the front of the hook. The yarn is then picked out with a needle or pick until all the windings are gone and there is a mass of individual fibers. When the yarn is completely shredded, the fly is then shaped in a ball to resemble a berry of roe. In fishing critical situations, where the water is very clear, small yarn flies can be tied on small hooks to represent a single salmon egg.

In some cases anglers mash pieces of roe, add a small amount of water in a bottle, and keep the yarn flies in this solution until they are ready to fish. It is messier than using fresh roe, but steelies readily hit this combination because the angler has both sight and smell stimuli working for him.

I often use yarn flies in spots where there are a great many snags. The cost of a single hook is minimal. These flies do not hang up often because the fluffed-out yarn protects the point of the hook. An effective way to fish these flies is to let them drag and tumble along the bottom on a completely slack line. They can become entangled in a steelhead's teeth like yarn draped over a bait hook. Fish will even pick up the soaked yarn flies that are laying on the bottom in still water. This is a good method to use when fresh bait is scarce.

Lures for Steelheads

I have used lures, almost to the exclusion of bait, ever since the appearance of the Cherry Bobber.

The important thing about the Cherry Bobber is that it is a spin-ner that floats. Before, you had to use metal spinners. These had the fault of sinking to the bottom and getting hung up while you were fishing the riffles and holding areas that steelhead prefer. Now there are many lures that both spin and float. You can even buy components and make your own lure and hook combinations.

Lures like the Flatfish and Lazy Ike can also be used effectively. In fact, any floating lure can be good for winter steelheading just as long as it vibrates or spins fast in moderate stream flows. A steelhead can locate a lure with a fast movement no matter how dirty the water may be. All fish have this ability to hear a lure in the water, as long as it vibrates or whirls. Even if I am using bait, I still attach a Spin N Glo spinner above the hook by threading the line through the center.

Bait Fishing

Fresh or cured roe has long been the standby for steelheaders who use bait. A berry of roe is formed by cutting a small piece about the size of a thumb tip. This piece of roe is placed in a piece of maline — a net material sold in tackle stores, usually dyed red — about four inches square. The roe is then gathered inside the net and tied off with thread or yarn. The excess netting is trimmed and a berry-size bait is left.

Most bait anglers prepare several dozen baits before they go fishing so they don't lose fishing time while on the stream. I prefer a single No. 1 or No. 2 short shank hook when I do bait fish.

A beginner would do well to use an old fishing trick. Tie a half-dozen short strands of red wool around the line above the hook. The wool should be about three inches long, only an overhead knot is needed. The wool should slide freely down the line and be allowed to drape over the hook and bait.

When a steelhead picks up the bait, the wool gets caught in its teeth making it almost impossible for the fish to spit it out. New steelheaders have trouble detecting a bite and using the wool helps greatly. It also helps the beginner to lip-hook steelies with bait instead of deep hooking them. A lip-hooked fish can be released.

Klamath River Steelhead

In the hundred or so years that anglers have been fishing the Klam-

ath, virtually every type of fishing tackle has been tried and tested for taking steelheads. Different types of tackle have been in vogue, but relatively few types of tackle are currently in use by the bulk of anglers who come to the Klamath. The angler who comes equipped with a reasonable amount of tackle or who adapts his current tackle to Klamath River conditions can expect to take his share of the steelheads on hand.

Various lures, baits, flies, and terminal rigs continue to come into style and lose favor with the anglers who fish the Klamath River. The visiting angler should certainly keep his eyes open to see what local anglers and those currently fishing the stream are using to take their fish. It is a good idea for the angler

Here are some key lures for winter steelheading. Each type is used in specific situations. The blob at right center is a yarn fly made of wool tied onto a hook and shredded to form a ball about the size of a roe bait.

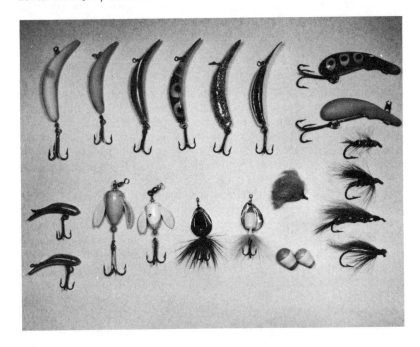

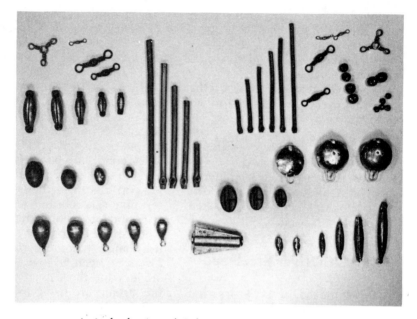

A good selection of sinkers is a must for proper steelhead fishing. Each kind of sinker has its use and serious fishermen should take advantage of what each type has to offer. Note variation in size and width.

to refrain from buying any particular type of tackle *before* he makes a trip to the Klamath. Tackle bought before leaving home may not be suitable for fishing the particular section of the river where there is a run of steelheads. The river changes character quickly along its course and from year to year.

It is better to have good, high-quality fishing equipment and to add to this equipment from the many tackle shops located on the river. Local shops will have whatever gear and terminal rigs are currently in favor with those who fish the river regularly.

There are only a few basic rigs used for taking the majority of steelheads on the Klamath and in the Klamath river drainage. The vast bulk of the anglers who fish this stream use either fairly hefty spin

fishing outfits or some of the better quality wind baitcasting outfits. Fly fishing equipment is built around rather heavy rods of the longer lengths fitted almost exclusively with sinking fly lines.

Most of the knowledgeable anglers who fish the Klamath a great deal use spin or baitfishing rods that measure about nine feet. If the visitor owns larger or smaller rods, he should not purchase a rig without trying his equipment on the river.

The main question the angler has to answer is whether or not he can work his equipment with the proper size lines and lures used for Klamath River fishing. Anglers fishing the Klamath use monofilament line that tests between six and fifteen pounds, depending on where they do their fishing. Lines that test between eight- and twelve-pound breaking strength are probably used more than anything else for spin fishing on this stream. The angler with only one spool for his spinning outfit should fit it with 10-pound test monofilament in order to fish virtually the entire Klamath River drainage.

Baitcasting reels are normally fitted with lines that test between twelve- and eighteen-pound breaking strength. Some anglers prefer to use monofilament lines or squidding line of good quality in the same sizes.

Fly fishing tackle is nearly standard for Klamath River fishing from the mouth of the stream to the headwaters of the river. A nine-foot rod that will handle a line of around 300 grains is ideal. Most of the better anglers also use shooting heads or shooting tapers thirty feet in length and fish deep in the currents for better results. Anglers who own rods fitted with the weight forward or with a heavy double taper line should not bother with the modern shooting head fishing techniques. The main thing is to have and be able to handle at least fifty feet of line on the rod that is used. In the vast majority of cases, the line should be a sinking line. Most steelheads in the Klamath will be hooked with flies that are fished as deep as possible.

As with steelhead fishing everywhere, the problem with tempting the fish is getting lures, flies, or baits down near the bed of the stream and keeping them as near the bottom as possible throughout the entire drift. The saying among steelheaders, "If you're not losing terminal gear on the rocks and snags of

Beaching a large fish is the surest way to land it.

the bottom, you aren't getting down to where the fish are holding," "is as true of anything that can be said about Klamath River fishing.

Terminal Rigs

The general terminal rig used for most lure or baitfishing in the Klamath River is the dropper rig. This rig can be used for both salmon and steelheads in almost every section of the stream.

Near the mouth of the Klamath, where most of the best fishing is done from boats, I prefer to use a wire spreader rig. Most of the commercially produced wire spreaders are made up of wire that is too stiff to suit me, so I make up my own spreaders from thin diameter piano wire. Most of the commercial spreaders also have the dropper strand too long for my tastes. I like the distance from the weight to the strand that runs to the lure to be about two feet or less. The strand to the lure should measure about three feet.

For general fishing in the bulk of the Klamath River, where weight is needed to get lures down to the bottom in drift fishing, I use monofilament line rigged with a three-way swivel — or with a simple swivel in the case of light fishing. The key to any of this dropper fishing is to make sure that the material used for the dropper strand is lighter than that used for the main fishing line or for the strand of monofilament that connects the lure to the rig. Then, if the lead weight hangs up, it can be broken off and the lure retrieved.

On my own rigs, I always use a large snap swivel to snap on the lead weights. I have found that if I tie the weight directly to the dropper strand, I am often reluctant to change to another weight in order to cover a section of stream properly. But with a simple snap swivel, it is so easy to change weights that I am far more likely to use the proper weights to get the lure into the right part of the stream. I lose a lot of snap swivels this way, but I feel that this is cheap insurance because having a large selection of weights and using them properly is the secret of taking Klamath River fish consistently.

Ultralight Rigs

Some of the choicest fishing on the Klamath River is ultralight spin fishing for smaller salmon and steelheads. Trying to get small, light lures or flies down to the bottom where the fish are holding is often difficult, however, with this type of light equipment. If you use even the lightest swivel with this delicate gear, the action of the lures and flies is almost certainly altered or destroyed.

A string of split shot can be used to get the necessary weight on the line in order to cast properly. A better idea is to score the end of a common pencil lead sinker and then pinch the slot closed as you would a split shot. Then the strip lead can be trimmed to exactly the right length to get the lure or bait down to the bottom where it will tap along gently. The pencil sinker is far less liable to hang up than is a string of split shot that adds up to the same total weight.

Try this rig for all fall-run steelies on spin rigs fitted with lines that test four pounds or less breaking strength. Some of the most sensational sport I have ever had in a lifetime of steelheading is tangling with

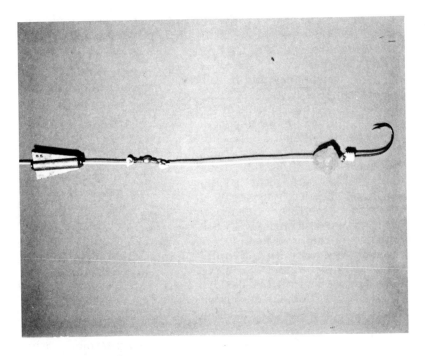

A popular combination for salmon is the sliding sinker rig as shown here.

even a half-pounder steelhead with tackle this light. I have had my best luck with this rig when using regular steelhead flies. You will hang up often with this method and lose some equipment on bottom rocks, but I feel that the cost is worth it for the sport involved.

Klamath River Flies

Although almost any fly used to take Klamath River steelheads will be effective, providing it is fished in the right part of the stream and fished deep, there are a few patterns that I have found to be particularly good. Fly patterns that are favorites on the Klamath River are also outlined here. The size, general color, and

conformation of the fly are far more important than the specific pattern being used. The angler who wants to be consistently successful in Klamath River fishing should have a good variety of flies, lures, and terminal rigs to offer the steelheads and salmon, rather than be limited by a few types of offerings.

For my own Klamath River fishing, I like flies tied on hooks of various weights. I rarely use flies that have fuse lead wire added to them to make them heavier. There is a practical limit to the weight of flies. I feel that if flies tied on heavy wire hooks do not do the job, it is better to move on to another spot. I do use some flies that have bead chain eyes added for extra weight and have found these to be very effective for getting the flies down deep in the current. I don't think that the bead chain eyes are themselves effective; the extra weight they add to a fly makes them useful.

I feel that the elements of size and type of fly are more important in steelheading than the basic color of an individual pattern. In my book, *Practical Steelhead Fishing*, I listed more than 150 patterns of flies that I've found effective. With a careful selection of patterns, perhaps a dozen or so would do. If the fly fisherman has simplistic leanings, he could do very well with just the Silver Hilton and the Fall Favorite patterns. Few anglers are this selective.

A list of thirty of the most popular flies for Klamath River fishing follows.

Nymph Patterns

Black Nymph: *Body:* brown chenille. *Tail:* brown hackle. *Ribbing:* gold tinsel, thin. *Hackle:* black sides, only.

Freeman Shrimp *Body:* flourescent wool. *Ribbing:* silver tinsel. *Hackle:* orange, palmered, cut off flush on top. *Wing:* orange bucktail, tied down at rear of body.

Red Nymph: *Body:* peacock hurl front, red wool rear. *Tail:* guinea. *Ribbing:* black tying, thread. *Hackle:* guinea feelers.

Wooly Worm: *Body:* black chenille. *Tail:* gray hackle tip. *Hackle:* gray palmered.

Comet Patterns

Boss, Orange: *Body:* olive chenille. *Tail:* gray squirrel. *Ribbing:* silver tinsel. *Hackle:* red.

Comet, Black: *Body:* black wool. *Tail:* black bucktail. *Ribbing:* gold tinsel. *Hackle:* black.

Comet, Brown: *Body:* brown wool. *Tail,* brown bucktail. *Ribbing.* silver tinsel. *Hackle:* brown.

Comet, Orange *Body:* flourescent orange wool. *Tail:* orange imapli. *Ribbing:* gold tinsel. *Hackle:* black.

Razor Back: *Body:* orange wool, black chenille along top of back. *Tail:* orange bucktail under black. *Ribbing:* silver tinsel. *Hackle:* white.

Yarn Fly: Double point hooks. *Body:* fluorescent red wool. *Hackle:* fluorescent red wool tide streamer. This pattern, if it can be called that, can be tied with any kind and color of wool. I have had my best luck with those tied of angora wool in bright fluorescent colors, primarily reds and oranges.

Bucktail or Winged Patterns

Alder: *Body:* olive chenille. *Hackle:* blue or black. *Wing:* brown and black bucktail, mixed.

Black Gnat Bucktail: *Body:* black chenille. *Tail:* red. *Hackle:* black. *Wing:* brown bucktail.

Coachman Bucktail: *Body:* peacock. *Tail:* red. *Hackle:* brown. *Wing:* white bucktail, jungle cock.

Dusty Miller: *Body:* silver tinsel. *Tag:* silver. *Tail:* red hackle. *Hackle:* guinea. *Wing:* brown turkey, mottled.

Fall Favorite: *Body:* silver tinsel. *Hackle:* dark brown. *Wing:* orange.

Fox: *Body:* gold tinsel. *Tail:* brown hackle. *Hackle:* brown. *Wing:* white bucktail.

Gold Hilton: *Body:* black chenille.

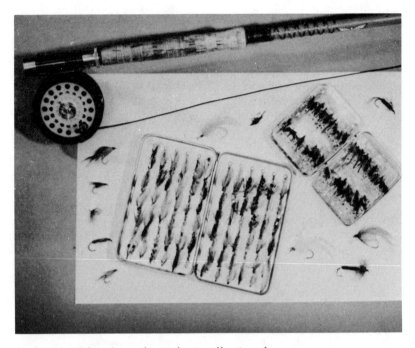

A selection of flies from the author's collection shows a great deal of variation in size, weight, and color. By having flies tied on hooks of different sizes and weights, the angler has a better chance to get down deep in the currents of the river. The place in the river where the fly is fished is far more important than the type of pattern used. In general, the deeper the fly is fished, the more steelheads it will take.

Tail: gray hackle fibres. *Ribbing:* gold tinsel. *Hackle:* brown. *Wing:* mallard flank, divided, short.

Jock Scott: *Body:* yellow silk, rear half; black silk, front half; silver rib over. *Tail:* golden pheasant. *Hackle:* guinea. *Wing:* brown mallard with peacock sword, jungle cock overlay.

McGinty: *Body:* yellow and black chenille. *Tail:* red hackle and teal. *Hackle:* brown. *Wing:* brown bucktail overlaid with white bucktail.

Mickey Finn: *Body:* silver tinsel. *Wing:* red and yellow bucktail layered, jungle cock.

Railbird: *Body:* red wool palmered with red hackle. *Tail:* red hackle. *Hackle:* yellow. *Wing:* black and white teal.

Shrimp, Orange: *Body:* spun fur, brown. *Tail:* golden pheasant. *Ribbing:* silver tinsel. *Hackle:* orange. *Wing:* orange bucktail, jungle cock.

Silver Hilton: *Body:* black chenille. *Tail:* mallard flank. *Ribbing:* silver tinsel. *Hackle:* gray. *Wing:* gray hackle tips, short.

Streamer Patterns

Black Marabou: *Body:* black chenille. *Ribbing:* fluorescent red wool. *Tag:* fluorescent red wool, wide.

Hackle: orange, under only. *Wing:* black marabou thinly tied.

Gray Ghost: *Body:* orange wool. *Ribbing:* silver tinsel. *Hackle:* peacock hurl, under only, long with white bucktail. *Wing:* gray hackle feathers, golden pheasant cheek, jungle cock eye.

Trinity: *Body:* red wool. *Tail:* teal flank. *Ribbing:* silver tinsel. *Hackle:* red. *Wing:* gray hackle feathers, jungle cock.

Yellow Marabou: *Body:* silver tinsel. *Hackle:* red outside of wing. *Wing:* yellow marabou, peacock overlay.

Hackle Patterns

Brown Hackle: *Body:* olive wool. *Tail:* brown hackle. *Ribbing:* silver tinsel. *Tag:* silver tinsel. *Hackle:* brown.

Gray Hackle Yellow: *Body:* yellow floss. *Ribbing:* gold tinsel. *Tail:* red. *Hackle:* gray. *Wing:* jungle cock.

Orleans Barber: *Body:* red chenille. *Tail:* red hackle. *Hackle:* gray.

Klamath River Lures

Lures for fishing the Klamath River are normally the same old standbys

A good metal lure selection for Klamath River fish includes a large selection of sizes and weights. Note single hooks on the larger salmon lures. Top left to right: Abalone Demon, Crocodile, Effzett, Skeena Skipper, Tee N Tee, Seadevlet, Dardevlet. Bottom: Bear Valley, Shyster, Abalone Demon, Mepps, Wob-L-Rite, Supper Duper.

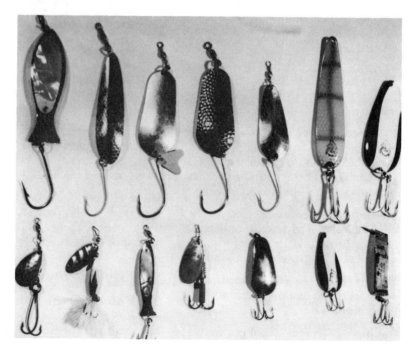

that take trout and salmon from any other water. Since the water found in the Klamath can range from fast-flowing riffles to quiet pools in the backwaters of the tidal estuary, the angler should strive to have a variety of lures and a variety of types of lures to offer.

Action is name of the game when it comes to taking salmon and steelheads. Lures without both action and flash simply are not productive. Lures that are not properly designed will react violently to the heavy currents found in the Klamath River. Within the range of a single cast, the flow of water may range from extremely fast to calm and slow. Under these conditions, properly designed lures with correct sectional density are necessary to keep the action going.

The wobbling spoon is an old standby in Klamath River fishing. Both salmon and steelheads will hit these metal lures. The key to spoon fishing is to have a variety of sizes and weights, since each spoon or spinner will react differently in water of different speeds and at different retrieve speeds. Metal spoons of all kinds will twist fishing lines. This is one price the angler has to pay for using these very effective lures.

Lures used in the tidal area should be very large. I also like to have single hook or Siwash hook lures. A big Siwash hook will hook over the lip of a larger fish and hold much better than any treble hook. When fighting fresh-run salmon, this can be particularly important.

I rarely use baits for any of my own Klamath River fishing because I have found that various lures are as effective as bait.

I am an inveterate tinkerer when it comes to lures and fishing tackle. My fingernails will be forever grateful to the Worth Company of Stevens Point, Wisconsin, for developing an extremely useful and simple tool, a split ring plier that can be used to open the split rings found on virtually every single lure manufactured today.

Klamath River Salmon

The equipment used in Klamath River salmon fishing depends on the section of the stream where the fishing is to be done. For instance, a light spin or level wind outfit that might be stout enough to handle a salmon in some secluded hole or drift in the upstream part of the river would be very wrong for fishing among the throng of boats that gather near the mouth of the river during the summer and early fall. When there are a lot of other lines in the water, the salmon fisherman wants very strong tackle so that he can stop a hard charging salmon.

Many anglers object to the idea of digging in their heels and fighting a magnificent fish like a king salmon to a standstill with heavy ocean-type fishing tackle. But the salmon fisherman has to realize that when he is fishing in a troll circle, as is done near the mouth of the Klamath, he has to take into consideration the sport of the other anglers on the river. Nothing is more irksome than to have a light tackle fisherman get a hookup and then to have an average-sized salmon tear all over the lagoon, disturbing the fishing of hundreds of other fishermen. There are plenty of spots in the Klamath River where the light tackle fisherman can ply his trade without joining the group or trollers or bank casters at the mouth. It is very probable that the

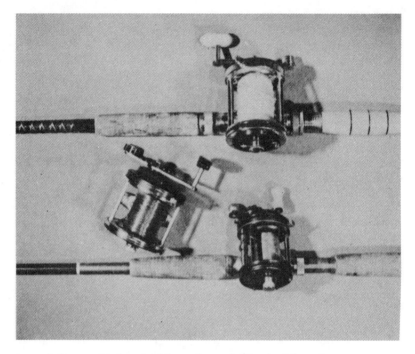

A sturdy boat rod is best for king salmon fishing in tidewater on the Klamath River. Braided dacron lines testing between thirty and forty pounds are best.

old-timers who will also be fishing near the mouth will give this kind of light tackle angler a bad time if he tries to fight a fish all over the lagoon.

Tidewater Tackle

The angler will want to use fairly heavy tackle in almost every part of the tidewater section of the Klamath. The deciding factor here is the sport of other anglers in the same area, more than the fish's ability to break off tackle.

The standard rig for the boat troller in this part of the stream is a star drag reel fitted with lines that test perhaps thirty to forty pounds breaking strength. I normally use monofilament lines whenever possible, but I have found that with monofilament in line sizes over thirty pounds it is debatable whether anything is gained or not. I have had just as good luck here using a rig fitted with 36-pound squidding line. I have rigs fitted with monofilament up to 25-pound test that I use for those occasional days when angling pressure is down.

When fishing from a skiff or other small boat, a long rod is a nuisance, so I use short boat rods in most cases. I also prefer rods that have a top roller guide. With a roller guide, the salmon fisherman isn't forever replacing lines that have been cut by a scored top guide. And since there is very little, if any, casting done by boat trollers, I've found that fairly stout rods of about five or six feet are sufficient for Klamath

River salmon in the tidewater area.

The majority of anglers who fish from boats near the mouth of the Klamath use rods that are from seven to nine feet long. With a rod of this size, it is difficult to control a large salmon once he is near the boat and ready for the net. Most salmon here are hustled in and are still very green when finally at boatside. A short, stiff rod would allow these anglers to net a larger proportion of salmon.

Sandbar Fishing

The best gear for anglers fishing from the sandbar or the area immediately near the mouth of the Klamath River is the same tackle that would be used for surf casting almost anywhere. While a few anglers use extremely long rods of thirteen to fifteen feet for this fishing, the average ten- to twelve-foot rod is preferable. With a shorter rod, the angler will find that it is not nearly as tiring to cast for long periods of time. The big, two-fisted rods will wear an angler out with the constant casting and drifting that is done here. It is doubtful if the extra distance they are able to get from their casts has any value; these long casters will also end up hooking lines cast by anglers fishing from boats on the other side of the sandbar.

Spin fishing is a very successful technique to use in this section of the Klamath River. Some of the deeper holes are so big that even the longest casts can barely reach the depths of the pools. A metal wobbler or a fast revolving spinner is a good bet here. But if you don't score in one spot, be sure to keep moving until a run of fish is located.

It does not matter if the sandbar fisherman uses spin or level wind equipment for his fishing. Both are suitable, although the bulk of the fishermen here seem to prefer spinning gear. The important thing is to use lines that test at least twenty pounds or more. With crowded conditions, even 20-pound test line can be considered light tackle.

Bank fishermen line the sandbars at the mouth of the Klamath River when the runs begin in the early fall. Most of these fishermen use long surf fishing rods and fairly heavy lines. This is advisable because the tidal action in and out of the mouth, along with the heavy flow of the river currents, makes landing salmon and occasional steel-heads difficult for anyone trying to use light tackle. The angler can't expect everyone else to stop fishing while he fights a salmon to a standstill. I prefer to use the same 36-pound test squidding line on my surf rig. With this gear I can dig my heels into the sand and get a salmon, pushed by heavy currents, up on the bar in short order, so everyone else can go back to their fishing. The rod I use is a ten-footer that gives me all the backbone I need for these fish. I've never found the need for more distance than this size rod offers.

River Fishing

For general river fishing, I have found that a rod fitted with 15- to

Metal lures of smaller sizes can be used for sporty fishing in just about any section of the Trinity River. By most standards, the Trinity River is not a large stream except in the lower reaches. An angler can comfortably cover most of the water in the stream.

20-pound test line is about right. I generally use a nine-foot rod for this fishing. This length gives good distance for fishing the wider sections of the stream and I can still use lines that are light enough to let even a light lure or bait get down to the bottom where the fish are.

If I fished a lot from a boat in the main Klamath River, I would want a rod that was a bit shorter, down to six or seven feet. But since I usually use the boat only to get to the spots where I do my fishing, the longer rod allows me to control a fish better when beaching him from the bank. I use monofilament here on both spin and level wind equipment. The smaller diameter of monofilament gives more line capacity in the sizes used. A salmon will rarely wipe me out of an entire spool of monofilament, providing I don't goof and nothing else goes wrong.

Trinity River

Fishing conditions determine the type of equipment that should be used for Trinity River fishing. While this is equally true of any stream, the Trinity River has such a wide range of water types that it would take the equipment range of a sizable tackle store to have exactly the right equipment for every single type of water available.

I carry a great deal of equipment, probably more and with a much wider range than the vast majority of anglers. I use this equipment in my own fishing, ranging from delicate fly rods that get a severe test from the larger steelheads found in the Trinity to big meat rods fitted with level wind reels for reaching out over some of the broad waters, such as are found in Hoopa Valley after the first rains of the season. However, a few rigs will normally do the job in the vast majority of situations found in Trinity River fishing, regardless of the time of year.

Spinning Gear

I have found that a 7-foot Fenwick rod fitted with a Garcia 300 reel is adequate for just about all of the Trinity River. I carry several extra spools for this rig fitted with 6-, 8-, and 12-pound test lines. With this range of lines, this outfit can be used for all of the steelhead fishing and most of the salmon fishing in the Trinity.

I usually have a spool of 15- and 20-pound test line that I will switch to if I see larger salmon in a given area. However, the Trinity River is not really noted for the large size of the salmon that run into it. A five- to twelve-pound salmon is about average, with many chubs smaller than five pounds running in the early part of the season.

Fly Gear

If I had to choose a single outfit from my own gear to fish the entire Trinity River, I would go for an outfit built around my Fenwick FF 85 rod. Any 8- or 8½-foot rod in the hands of a good fly fisherman is an adequate tool for Trinity River fly fishing.

In my own fishing, I actually do switch from one size rod to another as I move to different sections of the stream. In the upper river above the mouth of the North Fork, I have found that it is best to fish with an extremely light FF 75 rod. In the upper portions of the river, the banks are brushy and the flows seri-

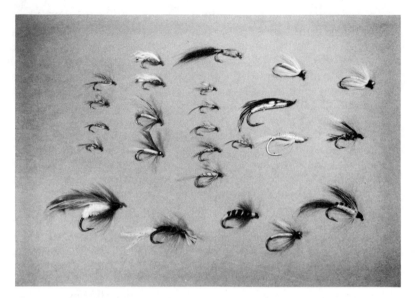

Close-up from the author's fly box shows that size and weight of hook are the main points in choosing a fly for the Trinity River. The streamer patterns shown here are excellent for shallow trolling during the fall and spring months at the lakes.

ously curtailed by the outlets from Trinity and Lewiston Dams. A big rod fitted with a shooting taper would be out of place in this section because it is hard to get much of a back cast. Here the premium is on worming through the streamside brush and then wading into proper position to make a cast.

Below the North Fork and in any of the gorges of the Trinity, I usually use my FF 85 fly outfit. This rig has enough backbone to subdue a larger steelhead. Trinity River steelies in the fall run are noted for their size, when compared with the average Klamath drainage steelhead. I have taken many that range well over the seven- and eight-pound class. These fish hold in rough water in the lower river and would be a bit too tough for a smaller rig.

When I fish Hoopa Valley, I usually switch to a FF 108 or FF 95 rod for covering the wider, deeper stretch of the valley water. It usually takes a fair storm to bring the steelies out of the first gorge between Hoopa Valley and Weitchpec. This means that the already sizable river in the valley gets even bigger and a big fly outfit is needed to quarter the stream here.

Trinity River Flies

Silver Hilton. *Body:* black chenille. *Tail:* mandarin. *Hackle:* gray hackle tips, short.

Thor. *Body:* red chenille. *Tail:* orange. *Hackle:* brown. *Wing:* white bucktail.

Fall Favorite. *Body:* silver tinsel. *Hackle:* red. *Wing:* orange.

Jock Scott. *Body:* yellow silk rear

half; black silk, front half; silver rib over. *Tail:* golden pheasant. *Hackle:* guinea. *Wing:* brown mallard with peacock sword, jungle cock overlay.

Brindle Bug. *Body:* olive drab chenille. *Hackle:* brown. *Tail:* brown hackle fibres.

Trinity. *Body:* red wool. *Tail:* teal flank. *Ribbing:* silver tinsel. *Hackle:* red. *Wing:* gray hackle feathers, jungle cock.

Boss. *Body:* black chenille. *Tail:* black bucktail, long. *Ribbing:* silver tinsel. *Hackle:* red.

Comet. *Body:* yellow wool. *Tail:* yellow impali. *Ribbing:* gold tinsel. *Hackle:* yellow.

McGinty. *Body:* yellow and black chenille. *Tail:* red hackle and teal. *Hackle:* brown. *Wing:* brown bucktail overlaid with white bucktail.

Mickey Finn. *Body:* silver tinsel. *Wing:* red and yellow bucktail layered, jungle cock.

Moth. *Body:* spun brown fur. *Ribbing:* gold tinsel. *Tag:* gold tinsel. *Hackle:* brown. *Wing:* brown bucktail.

Freeman Shrimp. *Body:* fluorescent wool. *Ribbing:* silver tinsel. *Hackle:* orange, palmered, cut off flush on top. *Wing:* orange bucktail, tied down at rear of body.

Rust Nymph. *Body:* rust brown, red wool picked out. *Tail:* guinea. *Feelers:* skimpy.

Gray Hackle Yellow. *Body:* yellow floss. *Ribbing:* gold tinsel. *Tail:* red. *Hackle:* gray. *Wing:* jungle cock.

Wesley. *Body:* silver tinsel flat. *Tail:* golden pheasant. *Ribbing:* silver tinsel, oval. *Hackle:* black. *Wing:* white bucktail under gray, jungle cock.

Other

Drift Fishing

Probably the fishing technique most associated with salmon and steelhead river fishing is drift fishing. The name refers to the way the terminal tackle is rigged and used. The basic idea is to keep the lure or bait drifting as close to the bottom as possible without hanging the whole rig to the rocks and other obstructions along the bottom, where both salmon and steelhead are most likely to be holding. To do this most effectively, the majority of terminal rigs are made to float; either the lure itself floats, or some kind of floating material is added to or above a baited hook.

Just about every lure ever devised to catch fish anywhere has been used with some success for salmon and steelhead river fishing. However, there is a family of lures that has been developed primarily for this kind of fishing. Probably the most noteworthy lures are the bobber series. These are shaped from plastic, wood, or other molded materials that float readily. Some of them imitate a cluster of salmon or steelhead eggs; some have plastic wings to make the bobber revolve; some are balls of yarn or other material that are attached to or draped over a hook, either baited or left plain. These lures are never, or rarely, fished alone. They are much too light to make decent casts and they float so easily they must be weighted to sink near the bottom.

There are almost as many ways of adding weight to these floating bobbers and other lures as there are lures. One of the most common is the cinch lead. This three-way swivel has a short length of surgical tub-

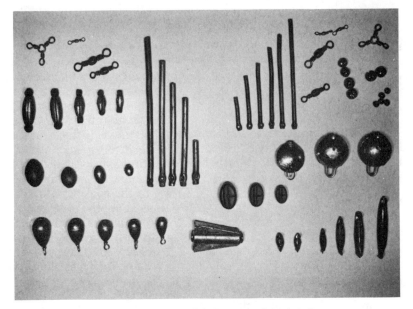

Plenty of different size weights and different styles of sinkers are necessary when drift fishing a big river like the Klamath. No single kind of weight is suitable for the wide variety of water found in the 200-mile length of river.

ing added to one leg; this is done by wrapping wire around the top of the tubing where it slides over one leg of the swivel. The lead used in this kind of fishing is normally solid pencil lead one-eighth, three-sixteenths, or one-fourth inches in diameter. The three-sixteenths of an inch size is the most commonly used. The lead is sold in coils; the angler can select the right length so the lure or bait can be towed to the bottom with just the right weight. The lead is inserted into the bottom end of the tubing. It will usually pull loose if it snags on the bottom, so the angler can retrieve his swivel and lure or hook.

The second weighting method is a variation on the cinch lead that becomes more popular each year. The lead tubing weight is hollow and is attached to a monofilament line trailed from a common two-way swivel. The same weighting adjustment must be used with these hollow weights, though much longer leads must be used in order to achieve the same weight as solid lead.

Some anglers prefer to use the bounding betty type of weighting, often the most snag-free of all weighting methods. The name comes from a trade item manufactured by the Luhr-Jensen Company of Hood River Oregon. However, any round weight can be used. The round weight is very often the only kind that can drift and bump along the bottom of very rocky streams. These weights are normally used for very slow currents. The fishing line runs to the rod tip running through the weight, but most anglers prefer to add the round weight to a length of dropper monofilament that tests less than the fishing line, which is tied to the swivel. If the betty should hang up, the line of lesser strength breaks and the angler gets the rest of his terminal rig back. The length of the leader between the weight can be anywhere from ten inches to four feet long, depending on the situation, though most anglers usually make the leader eighteen to twenty-four inches.

When an angler is fishing each new drift – and virtually no two drifts are the same, even though they may be within a matter of a few feet of each other – the weight must be varied. This is done by adding or subtracting from the length of the pencil sinkers. The weight wants to sink to the bottom and then tap gently along the stones. The tapping can be at any interval, but a slight nodding of the rod tip about every second or so would be a good interval for proper drift fishing. The angler must pay strict attention to the frequency of this tapping along the stream bottom because often a steelhead or salmon will merely stop the lure or bait and give little indication to the fisherman that he has actually had a hit. In fact, the experienced salmon and steelhead fisherman usually strikes whenever there is an interruption in the drift-tap frequency. This is particularly true of winter fishing where the cold water has made the fish less eager than they are in warmer water.

The theory is that a fish will strike this kind of bobber for three reasons: feeding, territory protection, and anger or curiosity. There are a few things the angler can do to increase his success ratio, especially when the fish are biting light. When using a bobber that is designed to be threaded onto the fishing line, he can add a bead just above the hook. This makes the

bead act like a small ball bearing and helps the bobber to revolve – if it's the revolving type. Most experienced salmon and steelhead anglers will use single hooks with a gap – the distance between the shank and the point – large enough to reach over the lip of the fish. A single hook uses less force to hook a fish. From an engineering standpoint a treble hook, provided all three points are engaged, is actually sixteen times harder to drive home. These hooks should be kept extremely sharp; no hook comes from the factory sharp enough for proper drift fishing.

When salmon and steelhead are biting light, it is also often a good idea to take several strands of bright colored yarn and tie it onto the line below the bead or beads so that it drapes down over the hook. When a salmon or steelhead mouth the yarn, they cannot readily spit it out again because the fibers of the material hang up in their sharp teeth. It doesn't matter whether lures or bait are being used; the addition of yarn is a good idea. Adding yarn to regular lures will kill the action of the lure.

The lures used most for salmon and steelhead are the spoon and spinner family of lures. The spinners used are normally the weighted type, with the weight in the body of the spinner behind the blade so that use of additional weight is not necessary. The stream angler can use much lighter tackle to cast these lures than would be needed for the more complicated terminal rigs. These lures are among the best to use in clear water because lighter lines are more effective. Because these lures represent natural foods, they have a universal attraction for salmon and steelhead and have a deadly success ratio with all the salmonid species that most other lures do not have. The strike given spoons and spinners by the fish can often be dazzling because the hit is so vicious.

Each spoon and spinner type and size will have a different action when drawn through the water. This kind of fishing involves more than casting at random. A successful spoon and spinner fisherman will study the actions of each style of lure in different kinds of water. For instance, a Bear Valley–shaped spinner would be a poor choice for fast-moving currents. This larger blade, when moved through the water fast, will plane toward the surface, while the fish are generally holding near the bottom. In this situation, a willow-leaf shape would

be much better. The opposite would be true for fishing a relatively calm pool. The willow leaf would have to be retrieved too fast in still water to attract fish and the Bear Valley or Idaho shapes would be appropriate. The same thinking goes for selection of spoon types. Heavy spoons are better in fast water and lighter and narrower shapes are best for still water.

The clarity of the water and the light level should be taken into consideration in lure selection. In roiled water or in very low light levels, the spinning or rapidly vibrating lures are preferred. Salmon and steelheads can sense lures and their movement even if they can't be seen easily. They do this by using the sense organs, called their lateral

A good drift fishing rig for winter fishing in the Trinity River. Hooks with more than one point on them may not be used from the middle of May through November in the Trinity or its tributary streams.

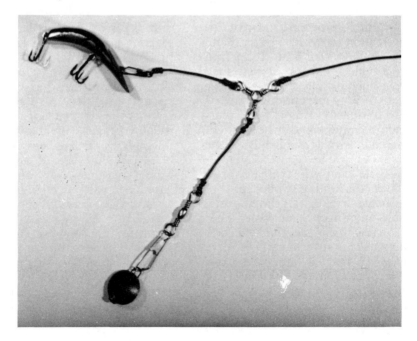

*A good selection of spoons and spinners will serve the angler
well. Note the spoons with single hooks at top left.*

lines, that run down their sides from head to tail. (This sense can be compared with a dog's sense of smell. A dog may not trust what it sees, but it always trusts what it smells.) Even when lures are very visible to salmon and steelheads, they will often make a single pass beside the lures to make certain it is something desirable before they actually hit the offering. They trust this sense, which is probably a thrumming sensation. What this means to the angler is that if fish are constantly following and making passes at his lures without actually hitting, there is something that is not just right about that particular lure. It could be color or size, but more probably the lure isn't thrumming in the way the fish want it to.

In the majority of river fishing situations, anglers will find they are faced with a very complicated set of currents. Even in a single drift and retrieve situation there may be many currents that are either fast or slow, changing in direction, and going in an upward or downward direction.

Lure manufacturers claim their spoons and spinners are designed so they will not twist the line. This is an impossibility. When faced with a variety of currents, the lure action will vary enough to cause some line twist. To avoid this, most salmon and steelhead fishermen with experience use an antitwist device. This can be a keel weight or a keel of plastic, but it is most often the same pencil lead system used by the drift fisherman. With these properly rigged and weighted, line twist is still there, but it is concentrated in the leader section and not transmitted up the entire length of the line. All the angler has to do is check his leader frequently enough so he can change it before the line reaches the fatigue point.

Hotshotting

One method of river fishing that has become popular in California and the other northwestern salmon and steelhead states is known as hotshotting, named for the lure type commonly used by thousands of salmon and steelhead fishermen. The technique was developed around the Luhr Jensen Hot Shot fishing plug. However, any other lure of similar design can be used. Most hot-shotting is done from a boat, but anglers are finding some success with side planers, a device designed to plane a lure out into the current while standing on the bank. The hotshot technique was first worked out by fishermen who drifted western rivers in double-ended boats that were rowed slowly to keep the lure or bait working behind the boat and near the bottom. This method is favored by most river guides. The double-ended boats are used because they can be floated in even the most difficult currents. However, in suitable sections of most rivers, outboard motors can be used.

The lures used in hotshotting come in several sizes, each meant to be worked at different depths. They also come in dozens of colors to allow the angler a wide selection. The lures are cast out behind the boat – the length of the cast depends on the depth and the current – and the lures and baits are actually backed down the river, working all the time in the current. The method is extremely effective: Salmon and steel-head seem to become enraged when these vibrating lures come slowly down to where they are holding in the river. It is not uncommon on a drift trip, when the runs of fish are in the river, to take dozens of fish in a single day. This technique also allows the angler to cover, in a single drift, virtually every spot in the river that can hold a fish.

For the angler who doesn't own a boat, there is a new product made by the Luhr Jensen Company that allows the shore fisherman to work every holding spot in a river. It is called the Hot Shot Side Planer. This product is designed on the same principle as the trolling sleds that use plastic planing surfaces to draw lures and baits to considerable depths in lake and ocean fishing. The side planer stays near the surface and moves away from the angler standing on the shore and can work lures up to 100 feet out from shore. If used properly, it can allow the shore fisherman to work lures and baits in all sections of a river, providing there are no obstructions. The side planer requires lines that test fifteen to twenty pounds. When a fish hits, the planer trips, allowing the angler to play the fish easily. The planer comes with two planing rudders: a small one for fast water and a larger one for slower water.

Jet Boats

Although a jet boat or regular prop-boat is probably the best means of access on the larger streams, many of the rivers in this guide cannot support boating at all. If the angler wants to get the most out of fishing the Sacramento Valley streams or many of the better sections of the Klamath or the Smith, a jet drive

A self-contained rig is ideal for the offbeat areas where facilities are few. The roads are rough and you often have to clear rocks before you can move on.

unit of some kind is almost a must. In the fall, when river levels are at their lowest, jet power is about the only way to get to the best fishing areas.

A jet boat is definitely an aid to fishing other Valley rivers. The Feather below the Afterbay outlet can be fished with just about any kind of boat nearly all year. This stretch is one of the premium salmon and steelhead areas almost any time of the year.

Automobiles

In any stream fishing, the automobile or pickup should be considered a piece of fishing equipment. Salmon and steelhead fishing can be, and frequently is, just as good fifty feet from the road as it is fifty miles back in the brush. The measure of an angler's success is how effectively he manages tactics and timing, not how far away he gets from other fishermen. If a visiting angler finds himself fishing alone, it is probably because there are few fish to try for. It will be a rare day when a visitor finds runs of fish the locals and river regulars have missed.

The Rivers – The Klamath

The Upper River

Oregon Border to Interstate 5

The maps with this guide can be used by the visiting angler. They are accurate as to mileages and show the access points to the rivers. To use the information in this guide effectively, the angler should read the boldface headings for individual sections of the lakes or streams. In many cases, information is concerned with the all-important access dope that anglers need to get to the water.

I have used the original contour maps published by the U.S. Geodetic Survey plus on-the-spot checking using an electronic bottom and fish locating device to ensure the accuracy of these soundings.

Access to the upper stretches of the Klamath River is difficult. All of the property here is held under private ownership and permission must be obtained. One rancher near the border allows access for a daily use fee. Right at the end of the border between California and Oregon there is a single access road, normally chained off.

Several sizable creeks flow into the Klamath in the short stretch to the Oregon border, including Shovel, Edge, and Long Prairie Creeks.

There are also numerous cold springs that burst from the towering rim rocks formed from lava flows in this area. This area is serviced by the Ager-Beswick Road, a good country road.

Klamath Above Copco

The flow in the Klamath River above Copco Reservoir is controlled by water releases from power-making operations in southern Oregon. Fishing can be dangerous in this upper river if the angler fails to heed the sudden fluctuations in the river. This problem was also a dread feature of the main Klamath River throughout the drainage, clear to the mouth, before the regulator lake,

Iron Gate Reservoir, was built. Iron Gate has now leveled off the flow in the Klamath below Iron Gate Dam.

Above Copco Lake the Klamath is a very fine trout stream and also good for the special Klamath perch. This area is famous for the annual hatch of salmon fly—a stone fly of large size. Every spring, usually around mid-May, this astounding hatch occurs and trout of large size are relatively easy to catch. These stone flies are as long as a woman's finger and they tempt even the most cautious fish to feed.

Copco Lake

Copco Lake is an excellent trout, black bass, perch, and panfish lake.

Copco Lake limits are common during the spring, summer, and fall months. The extremely high feed factor in this drainage, where insects hatch continually, is the reason.

Author shows off a very nice fish caught using a medium weight spinning outfit.

Trout are normally taken by trollers during the bulk of the season and the favorite lures are spinners. The local favorite is the Roostertail, but many fish can be taken with almost any spinner, especially when the ·salmon fly or case worm (caddis fly) hatches are on. Fly fishing is excellent with larger sinking flies like the Sack Fly or any good larger golden or dusky nymph pattern. The main thing is to offer the fish something that looks like a mouthful. The Klamath River is noted for the high quality of the feed that it contains; Copco Lake is a deep, food-rich part of the river system.

Black bass are taken by shore castings with plugs, using bait, and by trolling, especially in the rocky areas in late spring and early summer. The bass may go to well over the five-pound mark in this reservoir.

The perch fishing is nearly always good at Copco Lake. This little perch is really fine on the table; its eating qualities make up for its lack of fight.

There is a launch site and picnic facility on the south shore of Copco.

Iron Gate Reservoir

Two major tributaries to Iron Gate Reservoir enter the lake on the north side. These are Jenny and Fall Creeks, both very fine streams for the fly fisherman. Most of the trout are tiny, generally under the ten-inch size, but they are colorful little fish and hit well on small flies and on bait. One of the remarkable things about these two streams is the heavy concentration of caddis flies, known to most anglers as case worms. Nearly every rock in moving water has many of these worms on it; by plucking them off, the angler can get a ready supply of bait. The cases of these worms look like little tubes of rocks and pebbles; the worm inside is a succulent offering that will tempt most trout into ready strikes. Just split the case and thread the worms on a short shank No. 12 fly. I use a dark Wooly Worm fly to accomplish the same thing.

In the hot summer months, a heavy bloom of algae in Iron Gate causes some problems for the lure caster, but bait fishermen have little trouble taking bass, trout, and perch that are in this lake in hordes. During the fall, winter, and early spring months, the bloom subsides and fishing for all species is good and is done much like that in Copco. There are campsites, provided by the power company, and a good launching ramp along the north shore at Iron Gate Reservoir. Like Copco Lake, Iron Gate Reservoir is an extremely scenic lake with massive rim rocks looming over the skyline and forested shoreline. During the summer, some water skiing is done and the surface waters are warm enough for swimming. Iron Gate is a fine place to take the entire family for an outing, especially during the summer, when the water is warm and the days are balmy rather than extremely hot.

The surface elevation of Copco Lake is 2,613 feet; Iron Gate is 2,343 feet. The fact that these two lakes and the upper Klamath River are located in what is known as the banana belt of the Klamath makes for ideal weather nearly all year long. Generally, there is less rainfall here than either above or below this area in the Klamath drainage.

Iron Gate Hatchery

A fish hatchery is located near the base of Iron Gate Dam. From this spot downstream for 3,500 feet the river is closed to all fishing for the entire year. On the county road that services Iron Gate Reservoir and the upper Klamath River, there are signs posted indicating the section of stream that is closed.

Bogus Creek is the major tributary stream to the Klamath in the 3,500-foot section that is closed. This section is closed to fishing from September 1 through the Saturday preceding the following May 30th. This stream runs mostly through private property, anyway. It is a very good salmon spawning stream that is important to salmon and steelhead fishing throughout the Klamath River.

Access

In general, the far upstream section of the Klamath River from the Montague/Ager Bridge to the Iron Gate Hatchery is not accessible to the angler unless he uses a boat. A rubber boat is best because floating in this section of stream takes a lot of experience. A good bet would be to hire the services of a guide. Al Kutskey, who has a lodge above the mouth of Willow Creek on the north side of the river, operates a guide and river float service year round. A day or two spent with him will allow the visiting angler to float the upper river with a measure of safety.

Almost all of the upper river is posted by land owners. Only a few spots allow access. Just below the spot where the river is posted against all fishing, there is a small turnout where anglers can do some fishing from shore. There are two fairly good riffles here and anglers can take salmon and steelheads in the fall, from October on, with spin, bait, or lure. This premium section of stream is generally not fishable from the shoreline without permission of the land owners in the area. Float boats may be launched from a bar on the north side of the river just below Iron Gate Hatchery.

Access is much better for the visiting angler in the area from the Hornbrook/Ager Bridge to Interstate 5, although this water is not as productive as that found in the river above the bridge. This section of stream can be fished from the north side only directly below the bridge, but on the south side there is a good gravel road, the Anderson Grade Road, that follows the river all the way to Interstate 5.

There is some private property on the south side of the river but the bulk of the stream shoreline is accessible from the road. A series of pools and riffles along this part of the river below the Southern Pacific Railroad Bridge can be fished with fly, lure, or baitfishing equipment. The area closest to the Southern Pacific Bridge is generally the best water for the fly fisherman to work. When the river enters a steeper canyon section as it nears the freeway, it becomes better for lure and bait fishing. Salmon and steelhead do not hold in this kind of water. Instead, the angler should fish here during October and through the winter months to find fish that are passing through on the way to the hatchery upstream. Both steelies and salmon will stop off in this area to rest for a short time on their upstream migration.

Dates

This upper section of the Klamath River is a very important area for both salmon and steelhead fishing. In the fall, normally around the first week in October, vast numbers of salmon arrive in this part of the stream. The steelheads are never far behind the salmon and by the middle of October both species can be found in abundance in the upper river from below the hatchery to the Montague/Ager Bridge.

There is even considerable spawning action in this area in the stream itself and in the feeder streams such as Bogus Creek. This means that the salmon and steelheads that do not go up the fish ladder into the hatchery are available to the angler in the river for a long period of time.

Interstate 5

Interstate 5 crosses the Klamath River at Williams Creek. The old highway, U.S. 99, crosses the Klamath near the mouth of the Shasta River. Between these two roads, access is good on both sides of the highway – for the entire distance on the north side and for a short distance on the south side. There is a large turnout and rest camping area where the Anderson Grade Road crosses the Klamath to intersect U.S. 99.

This area between the two major roads is primarily a spin or baitfishing section of stream, but several short glides and riffles are good for fly fishing. Again, this is not a

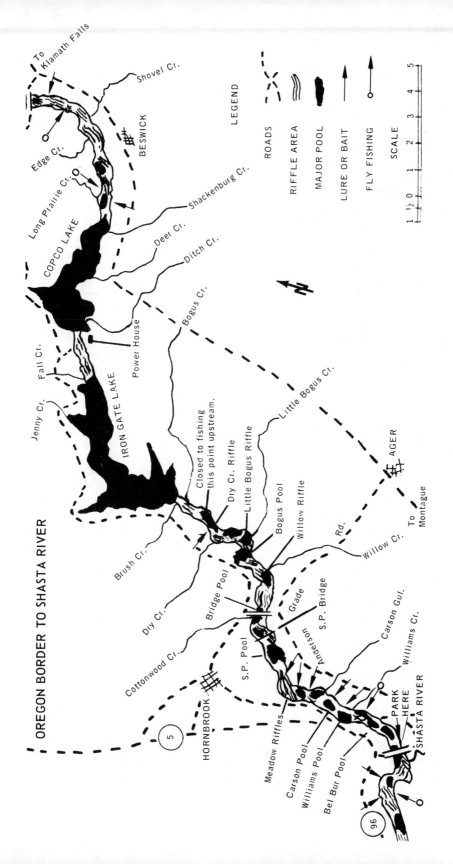

holding area for the migrating salmon and steelheads. In this 2.5-mile section of stream there are only a few dry creeks that have gouged out pockets where the fish can stop and rest. This area is serviced by a tavern at The Willows, just where the Klamath is crossed by U.S. 99, and by Bel Bur Resort.

Guides have about fifty different areas where they fish this part of the Klamath. In the fall steelies and salmon hold in this area in such numbers that virtually any of the riffles and small pools will have a good number of fish in them. The visiting angler will even see fish surfacing in the entire upper section of the river. It is a good idea to pay particular attention to the areas where small feeder creeks enter the main river. This applies even if the feeder stream is dry, since the feeder creeks normally have dug deep holes in the bed of the main river where the steelheads and salmon hold.

Equipment

Most of the fishermen who fish from shore in this area are those who own the property or have permission from land owners in the area. The equipment used should be fairly hefty for fishing from shore because the angler can expect to hook into salmon fifteen pounds or larger. Most anglers here use sturdy rods of about eight or nine feet and rig with lines that go from a minimum of 12-pound test line to an average of 18- or 20-pound test. With this kind of tackle, the angler fishing from shore can dig his heels in and give the bigger salmon a run for their money. With lighter tackle, not many of the larger salmon will be landed.

The basic rigs are common

drift fishing terminal setups with a dropper strand and the lure or bait tied on about two feet below the dropper. The bulk of the anglers fishing this part of the stream use bait for shore fishing. The most common bait is fresh salmon or steelhead roe, whch can be purchased in the area or taken from fresh caught fish. Many anglers prefer nightcrawlers for this fishing and they rig these worms on No. 2 and larger hooks.

One reason for using bait instead of lures in this area is that many areas of the stream are rocky as well as shallow. This means that in an average day the angler will hang up on the bottom many times. If the angler is rigged wih a simple drift fishing bait rig, the lost terminal tackle is comparatively cheap because the angler is only out the cost of the sinker and a single hook. With lures, the loss is much greater.

Whether using lures or bait, the angler should make sure to use dropper strands between the main line and the lead weights that test only about half the strength of the main line. Then, if the sinker hangs up on the bottom, there is a good chance that it can be broken off and the rest of the terminal gear saved.

In boat fishing here, guides have found that lures similar to the Hot Shot are perfect. Hot Shot lures are cast only about twenty-five to thirty feet downstream from the boat and allowed to work in the current, without any additional line or weights being used when the water is at normal level. The boat is then worked so that the lure is fished in the riffles and pools as the boat floats down the stream.

Fly fishermen can work this section of stream from a float boat, too. The angler merely anchors the

Some of the greatest thrills in the world can be found here between the Shasta and Scott rivers.

boat in one of the many riffles in this section of stream and fishes as though he were wading. When he has worked a section of stream with either flies or bait, all he need do is up the anchor and drift down to the next holding section.

Shasta to Scott River

Shasta Riffles

Some excellent fly and spin fishing water, called Shasta Riffles, can be found on the south side of the river immediately below the mouth of the Shasta River. No fishing is allowed for 250 feet up and downstream from the mouth of the Shasta River from September 1 through October 31 because huge numbers of salmon and steelheads hold here to rest, preparatory to migrating up this major feeder stream. But the water below and above this point is excellent—especially for fly fishing.

To reach this series of riffles and glides, park on U.S. 99 and descend the short distance to the Shasta River. There is a large turnout where a car may be parked on the east side of U.S. 99 a few hundred feet from where the highway crosses the Klamath. The riffles and glides can be reached by wading across the Shasta River and heading downstream on the south side. From the north side of the river, most of the fishing water can only be worked with spin or baitfishing gear. This area is also very brushy.

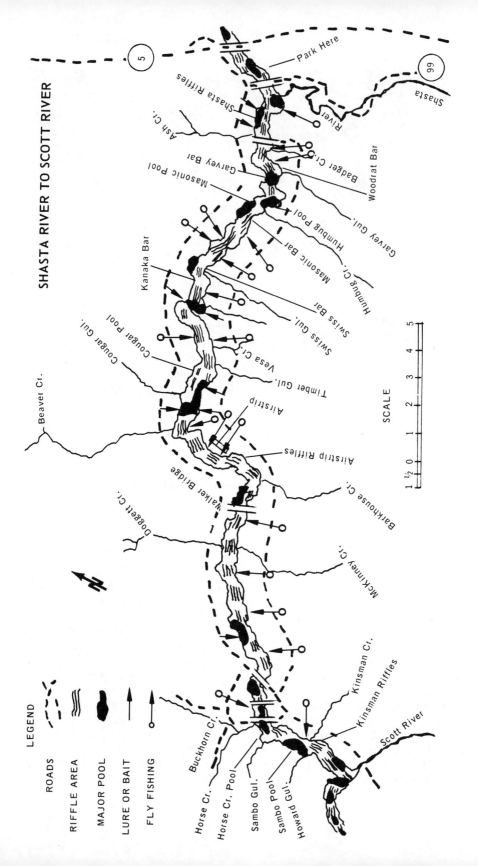

SHASTA RIVER TO SCOTT RIVER

LEGEND

ROADS

RIFFLE AREA

MAJOR POOL

LURE OR BAIT

FLY FISHING

SCALE

1 ½ 0   1   2   3   4   5

Beaver Cr.

Doggett Cr.

Buckhorn Cr.

Horse Cr.

Horse Cr. Pool

Sambo Gul.

Sambo Pool

Howard Gul.

Scott River

Kinsman Riffles

Kinsman Cr.

McKinney Cr.

Barkhouse Cr.

Walker Bridge

Airstrip Riffles

Airstrip

Timber Gul.

Vesa Cr.

Cougar Pool

Cougar Gul.

Kanaka Bar

Swiss Bar

Swiss Gul.

Humbug Cr.

Masonic Bar

Humbug Pool

Masonic Pool

Garvey Gul.

Woodrat Bar

Garvey Bar

Badger Cr.

Ash Cr.

Shasta Riffles

Park Here

Shasta River

Shasta

5

96

Ash Creek Bridge

One of the most interesting and important areas of the Klamath River is fished from the Ash Creek Bridge to the Walker Bridge. A good gravel road, which I have called the South Side Road, services this part of the Klamath. The road is 19 miles long between Ash Creek and the spot at Horse Creek where it again joins the main Klamath River road, Highway 96.

Virtually all of these 19 miles of water are fishable from the South Side Road but only a few spots are good from the Highway 96 side on the north. There are several rough campsites on the south side and one forest service campground located 3.5 miles below Ash Creek on the north side. A river guide, Robert Clyburn, who lives at Ash Creek can supply information and bait.

Woodrat Bar

The first notable spot in this section of the river is two miles below Ash Creek. This is Woodrat Hole and Riffle. Woodrat Hole is very deep and can only be fished from a few spots near the top and bottom of the hole because of the amount of streamside brush. Woodrat Riffle, however, is a series of three reasonably shallow riffles that can be fished well with fly fishing gear or

This is what steelhead fishermen from all over the world come to the Klamath every year to find. Fighting steelheads like this one pour into the river to supply some of the finest fall-run steelhead fishing. In a big river like the Klamath, even here at Woodrat Riffle, you have to use long fly rods and deep sinking fly lines to get down to the fish.

with lighter spin or baitfishing equipment. This is an excellent spot to fish after the first of October. It is primarily a steelhead fishing spot and I have taken some nice limits of steelies here. Good rough campsites will be found on the lower end of Woodrat Bar located in a stand of large pines adjacent to the riffles.

Humbug Creek

The next spot on this road is 3.5 miles downstream from Ash Creek at Humbug Creek. Humbug Pool is a large, fairly slow-moving pool where spin and bait fishing is good. In the late fall many steelheads hold in this pool waiting to enter Humbug Creek on the south side of the river to spawn during the wet months.

The best place for the fly fisherman is in Humbug Glide at the downstream end of the pool itself. There is a long slow glide that is perfect for fly fishing from the smooth gravel bar at the lower end of the pool. Deep wading is not necessary here, but the angler should cast as far across the stream as he can for best results with fly fishing gear.

Masonic Bar

The dredger tailings at Masonic Bar 6.5 miles below Ash Creek have some excellent rough campsites. The tailings have piled up in such a way that they have formed a good series of fly riffles interspersed with some good spin and baitfishing pools. Also, a half mile below Masonic Bar are Swiss Bar and Swiss Creek, where more short fly riffles and good pools can be fished. These spots are not holding water, but the river alternately pinches down and then spreads out, so that relatively short casts will allow the angler to cover any resting steelies that may be in this section of stream.

Timber Gulch

At Timber Gulch and Vesa Creek, 11.5 miles downstream from Ash Creek, there are some short riffles and another long, deep pool much like the Humbug Pool. Fly fishing is excellent in the lower two-thirds of this deep pool for the angler who can handle a long cast. Spin and bait fishing is good in the end of the pool. Steelies hold in this particular pool much better than in most sections of the river; the pool is relatively unproductive in the slower section. It is much better fished where the water begins to slow down from the upstream riffle and where it again speeds up before entering the downstream riffle.

Cougar Pool

About a half-mile below Vesa Creek is Cougar Pool, named for Cougar Gulch on the north side of the river. This pool is actually a series of deep pools where steelhead and salmon stop to rest before migrating further upstream. This is primarily a baitfishing area where good steelhead and some salmon are taken.

Beaver Creek

Beaver Creek is a sizable feeder stream to the Klamath River. It enters the river fourteen miles from Ash Creek on the north side of the river. Beaver Creek is important because of Beaver Creek Run, located just above the point where the creek enters the Klamath. This run is one of the finest steelhead fishing waters in the world. Steelies hold in this glide waiting for Beaver Creek to rise so that they can enter the

Successful steelheading requires the angler to keep moving and try a new location until fish are located.

feeder stream to spawn in the winter and spring months. They hold here for such a long period of time that the angler can take them over a protracted period.

While flies, lures, or bait all work in this glide, flies are definitely the best method of taking steelies. The slow, gentle run of water at the lower end of Beaver Creek Pool is perfect for fly fishing with a sinking fly line and long casts.

To fish Beaver Creek Run, enter the stream from the large gravel bar two-thirds of the way down the length of the pool itself on the south side. A short line of willows is located on the far side of the river. Fly casting toward these trees should be done only after the fly fisherman has waded out as far as

possible. The pebbled bottom makes excellent wading. The angler should cast and retrieve as he works down the long run toward the mouth of Beaver Creek. Most of the steelies hold from the bottom of the first line of willows to the top of a second line of willows located closer to the mouth of the creek. Best fly patterns to use here are Silver Hilton, Brindle Bug, and Fall Favorite.

There are some good rough campsites on the gravel bar and in the stands of pines directly across and upstream from the mouth of Beaver Creek. Parking is available on the gravel bar itself.

Airstrip Riffles

Most of the river along the south

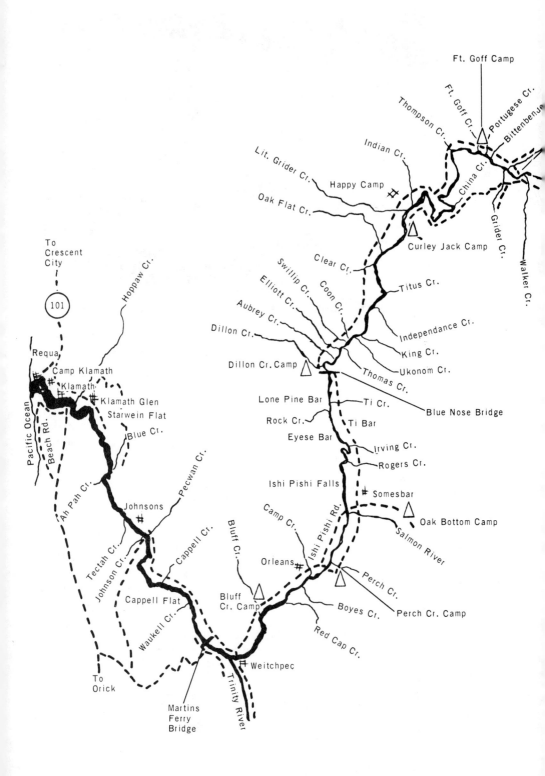

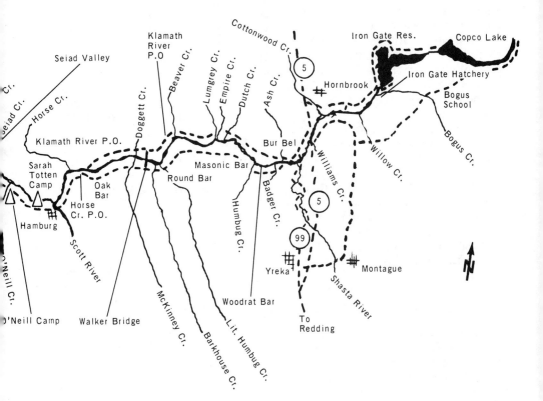

KLAMATH RIVER FISHING MAP

LEGEND

ROADS

SCALE

0   5   10

shore is posted against trespassing from Beaver Creek to McKinney Creek past the Walker Bridge, but there are two excellent fly and lure or baitfishing riffles at the paved airstrip located below Beaver Creek on the south side of the river. Do not park on or near the airstrip. Instead, park on the turnouts on the road and hike across the airstrip to the river. The first riffle is located near the east end of the runway; the second is located about halfway down the strip. Deep wading is necessary here and a wading staff is advised because the bottom in both of these riffles is made up mostly of stones the size of basketballs and larger.

McKinney Creek

Some excellent fly and spin riffles are accessible from the south side just below McKinney Creek about 6.5 miles downstream from Walker Bridge. These are not holding riffles, but they produce well when fish are migrating through this part of the river. The riffles are interspersed with some good spin and baitfishing pools as far downstream as Dong Creek and Oak Bar.

Horse Creek

Highway 96 crosses the Klamath from the north to the south side just upstream from the Horse Creek post office and resort. Between the spots where the highway bridge crosses and a second bridge crosses at Horse Creek, there is an excellent fly and lure riffle. This riffle and glide is about a half-mile long and can be fished from the north side for nearly its entire length. A third, forest service bridge is located just downstream from the Horse Creek

Bridge. A good holding pool is located just upstream from where the creek enters the Klamath. Horse Creek is a fairly large stream where steelies spawn; these fish hold in the deep pool. This is primarily a spin or baitfishing pool worked from the north side of the river. Cabins, camping, and a resort are located at the Horse Creek post office. An abandoned lumber mill and road system are located just downstream from the Highway 96 bridge.

Sambo Pool

Sambo Pool and a series of riffles are located 1.5 miles below Horse Creek. The access is good from Highway 96 on the south side of the river. Flies are good in the riffle, with lures and bait the best bet in the pool itself.

Kinsman Creek

About three miles below the Horse Creek Bridge are two series of pools and riffles: at Kinsman Creek and opposite Howard Gulch on the north side of the river. In both series of pools, the fly fishing is good, with deep wading hardly practical in the riffles and bait fishing and spin casting good in the pools. These are not holding pools. Access is excellent from Highway 96.

Another series of pools with good access is located four miles below the Horse Creek Bridge.

Actually, the section of the Klamath River between the Shasta and Scott Rivers can have some steelies in it virtually any time of the year. But the fall through early winter season is the peak of steelheading action during most years' runs.

Scott River

The section of the Klamath River immediately near the mouth of the Scott River is one of the most popular fishing spots on the entire river. Salmon and steelheads hold in the deeper water near the mouth of the Scott in large numbers. For this reason, the Department of Fish and Game has made it illegal to fish 250 feet up and downstream from the point where the Scott enters the main Klamath River. This closure, mainly to protect the upstream migrating king salmon, lasts from September 1 through October 31.

There are several excellent productive pools, glides, and riffles within a short distance of the mouth of the Scott River. From one mile above the mouth of the Scott to 2.5 miles below, these good holding spots are readily accessible from Highway 96. Virtually all of these pools and riffles are good fishing spots, but the mouths of feeder streams in this area are particularly productive. These include Tom Martin Creek, Macks Creek, and Jim and Mill Creeks.

Macks Creek Pool and Riffle is located near the south end of the town of Hamburg. It is reached

Here an angler plays a good salmon that hit a deep-fished bait. The Scott offers several miles of excellent fishing. The area is noted as a gathering place for both fish and fishermen.

SCOTT RIVER TO KANAKA CREEK

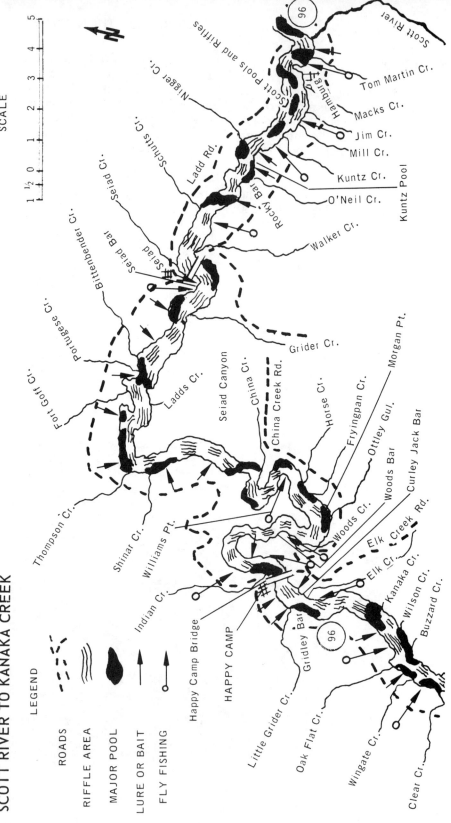

LEGEND

ROADS

RIFFLE AREA

MAJOR POOL

LURE OR BAIT

FLY FISHING

SCALE

1 1½ 0 1 2 3 4 5

Anglers score in these storied waters near the mouth of the Scott River. Here an angler plays a good salmon that hit a deep-fished bait. The deep runs of water immediately below the mouth of the Scott offer several miles of excellent fishing. The area is noted as a gathering place for fish and fishermen.

from Highway 96 by scaling the bank to reach the river. To approach this section directly, the angler must get permission from private land owners. It can also be reached by working up or down river. This is a good fly riffle and the pool is excellent for spin or bait fishing.

Jim Creek Pool and Riffle is located 2.5 miles below the mouth of the Scott River. This is another excellent fly riffle with the pool again good for spin or bait fishing. The access here is from Highway 96, which parallels the river. It is necessary to scale the streamside bank to reach this section.

Mill Creek Riffle is located 3.5 miles downstream from the mouth of the Scott. It is an excellent riffle for fly fishing because even a short cast will quarter the stream here. The riffle is located on the downstream side of the creek mouth; Mill Creek Pool is located upstream from the mouth of Mill Creek. The lower two-thirds of this pool is excellent for spin or bait fishing. Steelheads hold here before heading upstream, which makes them available to the fisherman for a long part of the season.

The Central Klamath

Kuntz Creek

From Kuntz Creek to Rocky Bar, the river is very accessible from Highway 96, which closely parallels the river. Several good glides and pools interspersed with deep riffles are visible from the road. There are many pullouts on the highway where the angler can park his car and work his way down to fish the river. There is some private posted property where permission is required to get stream access. Much of the property runs through Forest Service land and access is open to everyone. A forest service camp is located at O'Neil Creek near Rocky Bar where the Klamath makes a big loop to the north. Some of the access to the pools and riffles on the Rocky Bar section is through private property, but access is available working down or up stream from the bar. This is an excellent area for aboth the fly and the spin fisherman, but wading is tricky.

The pools on the bend of Rocky Bar are holding water where steelies hold for long periods of time before heading upstream. Most of the deeper pools in this section are fishable only with spin or baitfishing gear. Fishing these deep pools is a delicate business and the angler who works right along the bottom with either fresh roe or deep running lures will take the most fish. Landing fish can be difficult because the side of the stream drops off sharply, so a long-handled net should be taken when fishing this area.

The entire river can be fished directly from Highway 96 between O'Neil Creek to Rocky Bar. There are many turnouts where the angler can park his car. There are over twenty series of pools and riffles visible from the highway that are good for either fly or spin and bait fishing. The mouths of feeder streams in the area, normally dry during the fall fishing season, are still good bets because the dredging action of these feeders during the wet months piles up stones and debris in the main river and gouges out good holding pools.

Walker Creek and Seiad Bar

Just below Walker Creek, Highway 96 crosses the Klamath to the north side. There are two important fishing areas here. An access road to the outside of Seiad Bar takes off just before the road crosses the river at Walker Creek. This is the Walker Creek Road. The fisherman should take this turnoff and then, instead of following the main road, take the first turnoff to the right, about fifty feet from the intersection of the Walker Creek Road and Highway 96. This road leads along the outside bend of Seiad Bar.

About 1.5 miles further down, the road comes back to the river. A series of good riffles and pools are fishable from here and some rough campsites are available just beside the road. The road begins to climb away from the river and most of the access from this point on is from private property that is posted.

Just at the north side of the bridge on Highway 96, there are several turnouts where the angler can park. The river on the downstream side of the bridge is one of the finest fly fishing sections on the entire Klamath River. To reach this long stretch of excellent water, scale the short bluff on the north side of the river and work downstream from this point. These Seiad Bar Riffles are numerous and in the late fall they offer some of the finest fly fishing in the world. By working down from this point, the angler can cover all of the riffles on the in-

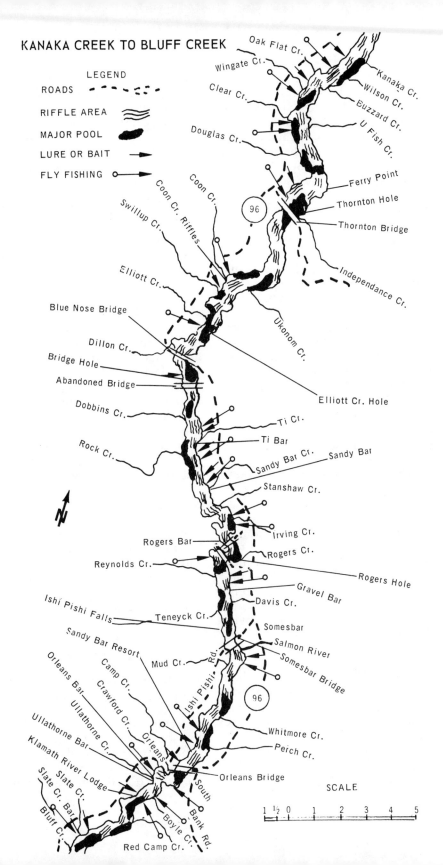

KANAKA CREEK TO BLUFF CREEK

LEGEND

ROADS

RIFFLE AREA

MAJOR POOL

LURE OR BAIT

FLY FISHING

Oak Flat Cr.

Kanaka Cr.

Wingate Cr.

Wilson Cr.

Clear Cr.

Buzzard Cr.

U Fish Cr.

Douglas Cr.

Ferry Point

Thornton Hole

Thornton Bridge

96

Independance Cr.

Coon Cr. Riffles

Coon Cr.

Swillup Cr.

Ukonom Cr.

Elliott Cr.

Blue Nose Bridge

Dillon Cr.

Bridge Hole

Abandoned Bridge

Dobbins Cr.

Elliott Cr. Hole

Rock Cr.

Ti Cr.

Ti Bar

Sandy Bar Cr.

Sandy Bar

Stanshaw Cr.

Irving Cr.

Rogers Bar

Rogers Cr.

Reynolds Cr.

Rogers Hole

Gravel Bar

Ishi Pishi Falls

Davis Cr.

Teneyck Cr.

Somesbar

Sandy Bar Resort

Salmon River

Mud Cr.

Somesbar Bridge

Ishi Pishi Rd.

Camp Cr.

Orleans Bar

Crawford Cr.

96

Ullathorne Cr.

Ullathorne Bar

Orleans

Whitmore Cr.

Klamath River Lodge

Peich Cr.

Slate Cr.

Orleans Bridge

Slate Cr. Bar

South

Bank Rd.

Bluff Cr.

Boyle Cr.

Red Camp Cr.

SCALE

1 1/2 0   1   2   3   4   5

side of Seiad Bar. The road turns away from this large bend in the river for several miles and access through the dredger tailings near the Lowden Mine is difficult from any section other than the north and south end of the bar. Spin and bait fishing is fair in the deeper section on the inside of Seiad Bar, but this is primarily a fly fishing stretch.

Ladd Road

About one-fourth mile past this bridge there is a forest service road that follows the Klamath back upstream toward Hamburg. The north side of the river is accessible from this road. Any riffle or run from Hamburg to Walker Creek that can't be properly fished from the Highway 96 side can be reached from this road, which has a forest service sign reading Ladd Road.

Lower Seiad Bar

Three miles below the Walker Creek Bridge, the highway turns back to run along the river again. There is a big turnout where cars can be parked. This is the lower, downstream part of Seiad Bar, where the angler can fish the excellent riffles and pools along the north side of the river by working upstream. There are about four miles of good fly and spin fishing water from this point to the Walker Creek Bridge.

Seiad Canyon

From the downstream end of Seiad Bar for 11.5 miles through Seiad Canyon, Highway 96 closely follows the river. This section of the river is very important because it is basically a canyon where the river pinches down and becomes deeper,

attracting steelies and some salmon to hold in this area all during the season before heading out into the relatively shallow section of Seiad Bar. The accessibility of this section of river makes it a good place to fish when low-water conditions are encountered on the Klamath River.

Riffles and pools can be seen from the highway. The mouths of feeder creeks like Bittenbender, Portuguese, Fort Goff, Thompson, and Shinar Creeks are the primary spots to fish, but virtually the entire stretch of river is good for bait and lure fishing. Fly fishing is also possible in this section. I've had my best luck here working from the rocky outcroppings with a weighted fly and a sinking fly line. I cast upstream with dark patterns like the Silver Hilton or a large Wooly Worm and let the fly sink deep in the runs close into shore and behind sunken rocks. I retrieve with the current. Normally, the deeper the fly can be worked in this canyon water, the more fish will be taken. Also, when working lures or bait, deep fishing is essential here.

The road leaves the river and climbs the flank of Cade Mountain 11.5 miles from the bottom of Seiad Bar, about eight miles upstream from Happy Camp. It returns to the river for a short stretch at Cade Creek where a series of fair riffles can be reached from the north side.

Happy Camp Bridge

The Happy Camp Bridge crosses the Klamath River from the north side, connecting Highway 96 with two important roads that service the south side of the river for the fisherman. These roads, the China Creek Road which heads upstream and the Elk Creek Road which

Limits of fall-run steelheads are common near Happy Camp.

heads downstream, lead to some of the finest fishing waters on the Klamath.

From the Happy Camp Bridge you can see some excellent pools and riffles. On the downstream side is the Indian Creek Riffle and Pool where steelies hold before going up this considerable feeder stream, which flows through the town of Happy Camp. On the upstream side is one-fourth mile of good fly and spin water that can be fished from either side of the river.

Woods Bar

The partially paved Indian Creek Road turns back to run near the river about 3.5 miles above the Happy Camp Bridge. This is the lower end of Woods Bar—a very important fishing area. An unmarked side road leads down to Lower Woods Bar Glide, an excellent fly and lure fishing run of water. This road can be spotted by looking for a house on the left, or stream side, of the China Creek Road and then taking the next turnoff to the left. The Lower Woods Bar Glide is just the first of a series of runs that stretches for nearly the entire length of Woods Bar.

A rough road follows the tree line on Woods Bar for about a mile upstream to the top of the bar itself. By walking or driving this road, you can reach some of the finest fly fishing water on the Klamath. Most of this water moves fairly slowly compared to most of the water in the Klamath River and it is ideal for fly fishing. Some short choppy riffles are also productive; spin and bait

The central Klamath features some of the finest water in the entire river. Spinning gear and fly equipment can be used on the many charging riffles found near Happy Camp.

fishing is fair in this area. A few rough campsites are located on the bar and near the pine trees.

Curley Jack

To get back to the river, a road heads downstream from the Happy Camp Bridge to follow Elk Creek. A short distance downstream is Curley Jack Forest Service Camp. Take the turnoff at the camp to follow the river. There is a bar at Curley Jack Camp with good riffles and pools. Steelheads hold here where the fast water of the upper riffle slacks off to form the pool below. This is an excellent fly or spin and baitfishing area any time after the first of October. Fish waiting to go up Indian Creek to spawn hold in this area un-

til the rains of late fall and winter raise the creek.

Elk Creek

A mile and a quarter below the Happy Camp Bridge, Elk Creek enters the Klamath. This is a considerable feeder stream which a large number of steelies enter every year. There is a large pullout where anglers can park. The fishing here is done above and below the mouth of Elk Creek in the long glide formed by the dredging action of entering the main river. Salmon also rest in the long pool below the mouth of the creek. A couple of rough campsites are located near the bottom of this pool, about 1.5 miles below the Happy Camp Bridge, just past a meadow with houses and trailers along the side of the road. The south road from the bridge ends here; access is very difficult from this point on.

Grider Bar

On the north side of the river, 1.25 miles below the Happy Camp Bridge on Highway 96, Little Grider Creek enters the Klamath directly opposite Elk Creek mouth. Grider Bar extends to the river and provides access to the north side of the long productive glide formed by the entrance of these two streams. The best bet here is to use spin or bait-fishing gear, although fly fishing can be productive, when the river is low, by making long casts with deep running fly lines.

Buzzard Creek

Due to steep banks, the next four miles of the river are nearly inaccessible from Highway 96 until you reach Buzzard Creek. There is some access where small feeder creeks enter the Klamath; this deep rugged water is best fished in most spots with spin or baitfishing gear. However, the fly fisherman can also do well by casting along the edges of these deep pools and runs with sinking flies. Working upstream with a short line is productive here.

Clear Creek

The next six miles of the river below Buzzard Creek are accessible in most sections. Fishing near the mouths of the feeder streams is the best bet, particularly in the case of the largest feeder in this stretch, Clear Creek. Again, this riffle and the Clear Creek Hole are holding areas for steelies that will migrate

up Clear Creek in winter and spring. Salmon also use this hole to rest during their upstream migration. This water can be fished well with either fly or spin and baitfishing gear. During early fall, and even during the summer, steelies and a few salmon will be found in this run.

Ferry Point

Access becomes a major problem downstream from this area. At Ferry Point, Highway 96 climbs away from the river, returning one mile downstream at the Joe Thornton Memorial Bridge. Thornton Hole, above the bridge, is a primary holding area for both salmon and steelheads resting on their way upstream. Early and late in the day, fish can be seen jumping; they can be taken here almost every day of the year. The best place to catch them is in the lower end of the pool, using spin or baitfishing gear. A short stretch in the upper third of the pool is primarily a resting spot where you have to entice the fish into hitting.

Coon Creek

The next accessible area of the river from Highway 96 is at Coon Creek, 26.5 miles below the Happy Camp Bridge. The mile of river below Coon Creek is among the finest on the river for the fly fisherman. A series of rapids is formed here; the bulk of the stream can be fished with shallow wading or from the streamside rocks. Work the side currents with the fly here as well as casting out across the river.

Between Elliott Creek and Dillon Creek, access is very poor. At Elliott Bar there is some excellent water, but access is through private

Rugged riffles like this one near Ti Bar are ideal for fly and light lure fishing. Fly lines should be quick sinking for fishing situations like this.

property and getting permission to fish is difficult. In general this area is fishable only from a boat.

There is a good holding pool below Elliott Creek and Dillon Creek Forest Service Campground. This pool can be fished with any kind of tackle from fly to bait. The salmon and steelhead hold in the deep swift water against the rocky bluff on the far side of the river. A short cast is required here from the bar below the creek.

Blue Nose Bridge

Highway 96 crosses the Klamath to the south side just below Dillon Creek, twenty-six miles below the Happy Camp Bridge. There are some good campsites on the north side next to the old road that follows the north side of the river for a mile or so just under the Blue Nose Bridge. An excellent spin and bait-fishing pool is located right in front of these camps. Between the Blue Nose Bridge and the abandoned bridge about one-fourth mile downstream, there is a big pool and a glide that is productive when fish are actively moving in the river. These are not holding areas and the fish are taken as they rest or move upstream in this section. Fish from the south bank here.

Ti Bar

Some of the finest fishing on the Klamath River can be found from the series of bars that poke out into the river near Ti Bar Guard Station. Generally, few anglers fish in this area, although some of the nicest riffles and deep pools on the river are located here. The bars are short and access to the stretches of river in between is not possible from the road. Good rough campsites are found on these bars for the fisherman who is fully equipped.

Sandy Bar

Downstream from the Ti Bar area, the next section that is accessible is Sandy Bar and Sandy Bar Creek. There are an excellent series of riffles and pools here, interspersed with very deep pools where steelies hold for a long period of time when the river is low. Both fly and spin or baitfishing gear can be used in this varied water. Of particular note is the pool directly above Sandy Bar Creek mouth. This is also a good salmon hole when the fish are moving upstream in September. Some good rough camps are located here.

Irving Creek Bar is an excellent stretch of river, but access is through private property. Unless you can obtain permission, it is fishable only from float boats.

Rogers Bar

At Rogers Bar the river makes a huge loop. The old highway follows the south bank, which is the best side to fish at Rogers Bar. The best access points are from the ends of the two new bridges that pass through the old gravel operation. The long curved pool is best fished at the top, the bottom, and in the shallow area directly below the mouth of Rogers Creek. The pool is very deep one-third of the way below the top of the loop and about

the same distance below. Salmon rest in these deep holes.

Gravel Bar

Road construction makes access uncertain below Rogers Creek. Gravel Bar, located two miles below Rogers Creek, is currently accessible from the highway and is a good spot for the lure or bait fisherman. At present, the access road takes off from Highway 96 at the upper end of the bar and heads down the steep bank. However, be prepared to find this area open or cut off entirely, depending on construction needs. This area is only fair for fly fishing.

Salmon River

At present, the only access between Gravel Bar and Orleans is at the famous mouth of the Salmon River. Salmon and steelhead can always be found holding in the deep pools above and below the mouth. Access is from the upstream side to the bar near the mouth of the Salmon.

Orleans

Highway 96 climbs away from the river; access is very nearly impossible until the road crosses to the north side of the river again at Orleans. The river at Orleans has some of the finest fly and lure fishing water in the world. The Orleans Bridge Pool is world famous as a steelhead fishing area. Currently, it can be fished from both sides. This pool has the habit of changing its course from year to year, but it is readily accessible and always holds good numbers of steelies. Long casts are essential to fly fishing success here.

During the peak seasons, most of the anglers fishing in the Orleans area will be working the Bridge Pool. This pool and the riffles above it are the most productive section of stream here, but I have found that I can do very well when the steelheads are on the move by fishing the long riffles downstream from the Bridge Pool. A paved road that heads downstream on the south side of the river provides access to these extremely long pools. I have named the two long riffles Half-Mile Riffle and One-Mile Riffle because they are located about this distance from the bottom of Bridge Pool. These riffles are actually fairly shallow pools with a moderate current that is nearly perfect for fly fishing. And, while lures and bait can be fished here, flies are actually the best gear to use in this section.

The best bet here is to wade in at the top of the long riffles and cast toward the north bank as you move downstream a few steps at a time. Steelheads do not hold in this water; rather, they move upstream. So, the problem for the fisherman is to cover as much water as possible. In a dry year when the river is running low, steelies will migrate upstream on the north edge of the stream. In an average year, however, they will normally move along a path almost exactly in the center of the river. The half-pounder fishing here is usually terrific for the fly fisherman. Some rough campsites are located a little less than a mile down the South Bank Road from the Orleans Bridge where a side road turns out. The sites are located in a stand of mixed oak and madrones. A road system along the bar here provides ready access to the lower riffles. A forest service camp is at Perch Creek a few miles upriver.

Ishi Pishi Road

After crossing the Orleans Bridge to the north side of the river, and before actually entering the main business district on this side of the river, there is a forest ranger station on the north side of Highway 96. From this point the Ishi Pishi Road takes off from the Klamath River Highway. A good run and riffle is located one-fourth mile above the Bridge. About a half-mile from the highway is Sandy Bar Ranch Resort. Guests at this resort can fish a big curve in the river for about a mile or so, getting good results with a combination of lures and bait in the deeper runs and flies at the heads of the riffles. These riffles are fairly deep and a long drift is necessary to get the fly down to the fish.

Bacon Flat

The next good access point from the Ishi Pishi Road is at Bacon Flat, where a group of homes and trailers is located. In this area the angler must drive along the road from one gravel bar to the next to obtain access. The river forms a series of big S-turns that bring it alternately from the south to the north edge of the deep canyon in this area. On the outside of these curves, the upstream or downstream access from the river bars is blocked where the river has undercut the rocky bluffs.

All of this water can be productive for the lure, fly, or bait fisherman. This area tends to run to deep, swift glides interspersed with deep but still moving pools. Because of this depth, both salmon and steelhead tend to hold better in this water than in the valley section nearer to Orleans. However, deep water is more difficult to read and changes character so quickly that the angler has to play his fishing by ear and change weights and depths of his casts in order to cover the water. There are few runs in this area where any one technique can be used for a considerable stretch of the stream. Access along the bank is rarely for more than a mile up and downstream from any given bar.

Between this spot and the Ishi Pishi Falls area, the Ishi Pishi Road climbs up and away from the river and access is almost impossible unless the angler gets local assistance. When the salmon are in the river, it is colorful to watch the Indians net salmon at the falls located near the mouth of the Salmon River at Somes Bar. The falls are located just above a bridge that crosses the river at Somes Bar.

North Orleans Bar

Back at the Orleans Bridge on Highway 96, the angler will find a series of access roads. They head out onto Orleans Bar off the south side of the road to service both the Orleans Bridge Pool from the north side of the river and the series of riffles, runs, and pools that can be reached from Orleans Bar on the north side. Access roads down both Camp and Crawford Creeks can be used to reach the famous runs of water along the outside of Orleans Bar. I have generally found that this side of the river is best fished with spin or baitfishing gear. Fly fishing stretches of great length are less numerous here than from the access roads on the south side of the river.

Ullathorn Creek

Downstream at the lower end of Orleans Bar, the highway comes back to run right along the river. At Ullathorn Creek there is an access road where some excellent riffles are located above and below the creek mouth. This road, which turns off the highway about two miles from the Orleans Bridge, provides easy access to the bottom half of Orleans Bar, which has some fine runs of water.

Klamath River Lodge

About three miles downstream from the bridge is Klamath River Lodge. The angler can fish several good runs from the resort access roads. By working along the north edge of the river, which is often rocky and tough going, the angler can fish nearly as far downstream as Red Cap Bar. This is primarily spin or baitfishing water, but the stretch of river is chopped up by short fast riffles where a fly can be used.

Slate Creek Bar

The next downstream access is at Slate Creek Bar, where an excellent short access road brings the angler right down to the water's edge. I have found that both steelheads and salmon hold about two-thirds of the way down the outside of the bar in a deep run formed below the mouth of Slate Creek. This is a holding and resting area for steelheads; salmon also use this pool to rest for short periods. In this entire stretch the angler should be ready to use every trick in the book to get his fly, lure, or bait down deep. The river drops steeply at this point and the water moves very fast, except at the very bottoms of the longer pools where few fish hold at any time.

Bluff Creek

About a mile below Slate Creek is Bluff Creek. The Bluff Creek hole is famous in this area as a major salmon holding pool. It is confusing to locate this pool since the 1964 flood changed the location of the mouth of Bluff Creek. Formerly, the creek entered the Klamath about three-quarters of a mile downstream at what is now marked as Aiken Creek. The Bluff Creek Pool used to be located above the mouth of Bluff Creek. Now it is located downstream from the new mouth of Bluff Creek. To reach the pool, the angler has to turn off Highway 96 at a spot close to Aiken Creek and drive down the gravel bar. The pool is located behind a huge rocky headland that juts up to block the view of the river from the highway.

This entire Bluff Creek area is primarily a spin or baitfishing area. Some steelies are taken here just above and below the new Bluff Creek mouth, but spin fishing gear is much the better type of tackle to use, not only in the deep pool but in the rugged riffles and runs. Forest service camps are located at Bluff Creek.

Clearwater Gulch

At Clearwater Gulch about 2.5 miles below Aiken Creek, there is a good bar with three excellent rough water fly fishing riffles. Wading here is nearly impossible and usually unnecessary. The best way to take the steelies as they move along the edges of the rough riffles is to cast with weighted flies and sinking fly lines. Then work upstream, fishing from the rocks, and let the fly sink deep as it is retrieved with the downstream float. This fishing is generally good only when the runs of steelies are at their peak. Trying to land even a small steelhead in this roaring water is worth the special effort and techniques involved for the fly fisherman. There is a huge rock that juts out into the stream at the bottom of this stretch that is worth special attention. Both steelheads and salmon hold in the deep pool behind and outside this rock. It is said that in the past this was a favorite spearing hold for the Indians. Fish deep with lures or bait here.

Hopkins Creek

The spin or bait fisherman should pay special attention to the section of the Klamath River at Cavanaugh and Hopkins Creeks. Just upstream from the point where Cavanaugh Creek enters the river from the north side, Hopkins Creek can be seen as a gash that cuts a rocky path down the flank of the mountain on the south side of the river. Steelies tend to hold better and for a longer period of time in the Hopkins to Cavanaugh Creek section than they do in all the rest of this general stretch of the Klamath.

It is an truism of the natives that even in a low warm-water period this is one of the top areas in the entire Klamath River—if steelies aren't holding here, very probably they aren't in this section of stream at all. Access is down a very steep trail located directly across from the Hopkins Creek rock gash. This is primarily spin or baitfishing water. The deep riffles are few and difficult for the fly fisherman to work. I usually work downstream from the mouth of Hopkins Creek to the mouth of Cavanaugh Creek. Neither creek is marked on the road,

The Klamath is extremely scenic in almost all areas. This riffle is typical of hundreds found on the river above the mouth of the Trinity.

but the trail is one mile below Clearwater Gulch and 3.5 miles below Aiken Creek, which is clearly marked on the highway. The main thing to look for is the sizable rocky gash in the mountain on the far side of the river.

The Lower Klamath

Trinity River to Mouth

Klamath River Highway 96 crosses the river at Weitchpec on the Weitchpec Bridge. It heads south along the length of the Trinity River, probably the major tributary to the main river in the entire Klamath River drainage. At Willow Creek, Highway 96 joins U.S. 299, which connects with Redding and Eureka.

From the Weitchpec Bridge to the very mouth of the Klamath River, approximately forty-two miles downstream, there are important changes in both access to the river and the type of water. Upstream from the mouth of the Trinity River is a river of reasonable size with shorter riffles and shallower water interspersed with deep pools. The lower Klamath, however, between this point and the tidewater section above Terwer Valley, is a much larger stream at any season and the water is interspersed with fast runs pinched in between steep-banked shores and wide, deep, and swift riffles or runs.

Trinity River

Roughly 50 percent of the salmon and almost that big a percentage of the steelies that enter the Klamath River system cut off at the Trinity River and head upstream to spawn in this major stream. This means that the lower forty miles or so of the main river is the only spot that almost all the migrating fish come into at various seasons of the year. The lower Klamath also has the bulk of the important cutthroat and silver salmon runs. Above the Weitchpec Bridge one rarely sees runs of these species. But the angler is also faced with a much larger stream below this point and much more limited access to the river.

As a general rule, I usually suggest that an angler who wants to fish the bulk of the lower river and avoid the crowds that throng here use a boat to fish this lower forty miles of stream. This is the way I prefer to fish the lower Klamath River.

I try to be on the stream around Labor Day each year. I launch my boat at the mouth of Pecwan Creek near Johnson's about twenty-five miles down the Johnson's Road that skirts the north shore of the river below the Weitchpec Bridge. The huge gravel bar at this point looks like Coney Island on the long Labor Day weekend. In spite of the fact that Pecwan Bar will look like a small city at night at this time of year, nearly everyone on hand will take fish because of the huge salmon runs. I use my own cartop boat to get away from the crossed lines and crowded beaches in this area.

Weitchpec Bridge

For the angler who does not own a boat or who prefers to fish from the bank, the access points below the Weitchpec Bridge to Johnson's are limited but well defined. The first access point is at the bridge itself. A trail leads down to the pools and runs just above the mouth of the Trinity River. Many salmon and steelheads are taken here annually, almost entirely with lures or bait. Another trail leads down from the north side of the river behind the Weitchpec Store to a bar formed where the two rivers meet. Here you will find a combination of big, fast fly fishing riffles and spin fishing glides from the pointed bar at the mouth of the Trinity. You can fish both rivers at this point where the waters of the two rivers mix.

In order to reach the huge bar on the north side of the Klamath above and below the mouth of the Trinity, you have to scale the steep ridge. Both salmon and steelhead hold along this bar in the riffles and the deep pool at the lower end of the bar before committing themselves to moving up either river. There is a jeep trail down to this bar through private property.

Martins Ferry Bridge

The next downstream access point is the Martins Ferry Bridge about 4.5 miles below the Weitchpec Bridge. This bridge has a deep spin and bait pool below it. You can fish for about a mile in either direction from the base of the bridge. Fly fishing is difficult here.

Pine Creek Run

By crossing the Martins Ferry Bridge, the angler will find access roads heading both upstream and downstream. On the upstream side, where the Orick Road heads along the Klamath for a short stretch, there is a short access road that takes off toward the river about a mile upstream from the bridge.

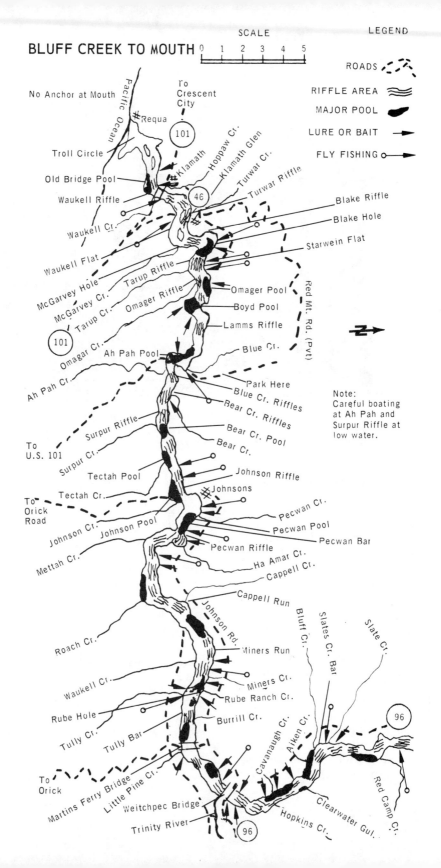

BLUFF CREEK TO MOUTH

Pacific Ocean

No Anchor at Mouth

To Crescent City

Requa

101

Troll Circle

Old Bridge Pool

Waukell Riffle

Klamath

Hoppaw Cr.

Klamath Glen

Turwar Cr.

Turwar Riffle

46

Waukell Cr.

Blake Riffle

Blake Hole

Starwein Flat

Waukell Flat

McGarvey Hole

Tarup Riffle

McGarvey Cr.

Tarup Cr.

Omager Riffle

Omager Pool

Boyd Pool

Lamms Riffle

101

Omagar Cr.

Ah Pah Pool

Blue Cr.

Red Mt. Rd. (Pvt)

Ah Pah Cr.

Park Here

Blue Cr. Riffles

Bear Cr. Riffles

Note:
Careful boating
at Ah Pah and
Surpur Riffle at
low water.

Surpur Riffle

Bear Cr. Pool

To U.S. 101

Surpur Cr.

Bear Cr.

Tectah Pool

Johnson Riffle

Tectah Cr.

Johnsons

To Orick Road

Pecwan Cr.

Johnson Ct.

Pecwan Pool

Pecwan Bar

Johnson Pool

Mettah Cr.

Pecwan Riffle

Ha Amar Cr.

Cappell Cr.

Cappell Run

Roach Cr.

Johnson Rd.

Bluff Cr.

Slates Cr.

Slate Cr.

96

Miners Run

Waukell Cr.

Miners Cr.

Rube Ranch Cr.

Rube Hole

Slates Cr. Bar

Burrill Cr.

Tully Cr.

Tully Bar

To Orick

Cavanaugh Cr.

Aiken Cr.

Red Camp Cr.

Martins Ferry Bridge

Little Pine Cr.

Weitchpec Bridge

Clearwater Gul.

Trinity River

96

Hopkins Cr.

This angler shows a practical way to tote a brace of larger fish from one place to another while working the length of a stream. A pair, or a limit, can often weigh thirty or forty pounds.

This road deadends at Little Pine Creek. Cars may be parked here and the Pine Creek Run can be fished after a short hike down Pine Creek. Both salmon and steelheads hold along the protected sides of the rubble pile built up by the creek just below the point where it enters the Klamath.

Tully Creek Run

The same type of stream access can be found at the mouth of Tully Creek about two miles downstream from the Martins Ferry Bridge. At Tully Creek there are several excellent rough camps and it is only a short walk down to the Tully Creek Run. Here, as in the case of most active feeders, the creek has piled riprap into the main river, which breaks up the main currents of the Klamath and offers protection for resting steelies and salmon. This road deadends on private property and the only access from this point is through old logging roads that do not reach the shores of the Klamath. A few tiny creeks drain this slope but access is so difficult that few anglers fish from here.

Rube Ranch Creek

Back on the Johnson Road on the north side of the river, the next access is down a steep bluff. This is primarily spin or baitfishing water from the shore. The mouth of Tully Creek and Tully Creek Run below the mouth can be seen from the

Rube Ranch side of the river. Fly fishing here is difficult from shore.

Miners Bar

Something special for the shore fisherman is found during the runs at Miners Bar. I have rarely failed to take steelies from the waters of Miners Bar after Labor Day. I have hooked a few salmon here, but this is mostly a fly and lure section of stream for the steelhead fisherman.

Miners Bar is formed by the buildup of rubble and gravel at the mouth of Miners Creek. This creek is well marked and is located 10.8 miles downstream on the Johnson Road along the north bank below Martins Ferry Bridge. On the bluff overlooking the river, just upstream from the mouth of the creek, is a large flat where autos may be parked. Access is by walking down a fairly rough road that leads to Miners Bar.

I have had my best luck fly fishing with deep sinking flies in the glide below the mouth of Miners Creek. I seldom find it necessary to use weighted flies here except during periods of high water. I even use light spin fishing gear to fish this stretch during high water because it seldom fails to hold a supply of steelies after the first of September. I vary the amount of weight until I can get to the bottom and have bait or lure working just off the bottom. This water below the mouth of the Miner Run is a glide of water rather than an identifiable riffle as such.

The gouged-out pool just at the mouth of Miners Creek is best fished with lures and bait. This spot often produces salmon, although they generally do not hold here but rest up under the upstream lip of the pool. Another good fly run, more of a riffle most years, can be found just upstream from the creek mouth. This I rate as a fair fly drift. It is very short in length before it deepens into lure and bait drifting water less than a few hundred feet downstream. Wading in this whole area is very good most years.

Cappell Run

I have never fished the Klamath River below the Miners Bar section by climbing down from the road. But I have seen many anglers who were stuck with bank fishing who descended the bluff either at Cappell Creek or from a turnout located about a quarter of a mile below Cappell Creek. I normally fish this entire stretch from the bank but I reach the area by heading upstream from where I launch my boat at Pecwan Bar.

The runs of water from Cappell Bar opposite Cappell Flat, located on the south side of the river, are among the finest in the entire Klamath River. This is mostly a spot for anglers who can handle a long line fishing from shore or for bait fishermen who drift and cast with light spin gear rigged for bait fishing. The fly fisherman can make short casts after running a boat to the top of a glide. He can then drift downstream, allowing the fly to sink, and slowly retrieve. I have fished both ways and have come to prefer wading here because you can do a much better job covering the water. When the water deepens on one side of the Cappell Run, I get in the boat and go over to the other side where wading is good again. This whole run of water — stretching about five or six stream miles upstream from Pecwan Bar — is a complicated series of glides, runs, true riffles, and fairly shallow pools making one of the finest sections of the Klamath River to fish after Labor Day. It is the single spot on the lower river that I prefer to fish over all others. I call this the Cappell to Pecwan Run because it is such a complicated system that trying to name every feature would be impossible.

Pecwan Creek

Pecwan Creek and the gravel bar at the mouth of the creek are extremely important to anglers who want to fish the waters between this point and tidewater. The bar at the mouth of the creek provides excellent access for the fisherman who wants to launch a small boat. From a boat the entire river from Weitchpec to the ocean is open to the fisherman.

A tradition has grown up concerning Pecwan Bar. Anglers from all over the world gather in large numbers to fish over the Labor Day weekend. At this time of year the salmon are normally swarming in this section of stream. So, even though thousands of anglers may be fishing the stream in this area each season on Labor Day and the week or two before and after, incredible numbers of salmon and steelheads are landed both by bank fishermen and by anglers fishing from a boat.

The angler who uses a boat can also fish the riffles and pools upstream from Pecwan Creek because there is normally plenty of water in the river anywhere below the mouth of the Trinity River.

Johnson Pool and Riffle

Johnson Pool and Riffle is located on the river about three-quarters of a mile below Pecwan Bar. It is a favorite of both the salmon and

steelhead fishermen who launch at Pecwan. This is an excellent drift fishing area since the salmon tend to hold and rest in the depths of Johnson Pool in greater numbers than in most of the other holds in this area.

In dry years Johnson Riffle is excellent for steelhead fishing, either by drift fishing from a boat with bait or lures or fishing from shore with wading equipment. This is an excellent fly fishing riffle most years and steelies hold about halfway down the length of the riffle.

Tectah Pool

Tectah Pool, near the mouth of Tectah Creek, is a holding area for both salmon and steelheads. The silver salmon that normally run in the lower Klamath River in late fall are particularly likely to hold in this deep pool. King salmon and steelheads also prefer the resting area at the top of this pool.

The inflowing action of Tectah Creek at high water tends to alternately fill and gouge out Tectah Pool. The depth of the pool itself depends on the stage of filling and gouging at any particular time. But, generally, the area just below the mouth of the creek is the prime spot to fish this part of the river.

The boater should be particularly careful when drifting or running the section of the Klamath River between Tectah Creek and Surpur Creek. In low-water years there is a lot of rough water around Bear Creek Pools.

Bear Creek Pools

Bear Creek Pools are a series of pools interspersed between runs of fast water. The pools are often not difficult to locate because the entire section along Bear Creek Riffle is fast moving and broken by underwater obstructions. But this area, located about five miles below Pecwan Bar, is one of the prime drift and still fishing areas on the lower river.

The best run of water in this area is located just above and below Surpur Creek mouth. This is also the area where boating is most dangerous; the angler new to the river should try to get another fisherman to go along on at least the first few trips.

Just below Bear Creek mouth, the sand and gravel bar that has been formed is excellent for steelhead fly, lure, and bait fishing. The pool directly above the mouth of the creek is an excellent salmon drift and still fishing hole. The angler fishing for salmon from a boat here should have at least forty feet of anchor rope to get a good bite into the rocky bottom.

Blue Creek

Blue Creek is the major tributary to the lower Klamath River below the mouth of the Trinity River. A whole series of pools and riffles is formed near the mouth of the creek. An excellent access road owned by a lumber company services the mouth of the stream on the north side. Anglers without a boat can get permission to use this road.

Even when there is a big rain storm in the area, Blue Creek will normally run clearer than the main river. Both salmon and steelheads hold in the clearer water inside and just outside of the mouth of Blue Creek during these stormy periods. Blue Creek Riffle above the mouth of the creek is an excellent steelhead drift fishing area with either lures or bait. This is a regular stopping spot for steelies in the lower stretches of the river. Many steelheads and silver salmon hold here waiting to migrate up Blue Creek to spawn. Populations of steelheads can be found here anytime after the runs begin.

Lamms Riffle

Lamms Riffle is a mile-long stretch of water located below the mouth of Blue Creek. Steelheads and salmon hold in this area waiting to go up Blue Creek to spawn. This area, along with Boyd Pool along the north bank of the river, will produce both king and silver salmon and steelheads in the faster moving water.

This entire section of river can best be worked from a boat launched at any of the ramps on the lower river. The movement of the tides in and out of the river will affect the movement of both salmon and steelhead to a great extent from Blake Hole downstream. It will also cause movements of the fish in the lower river upstream as far as Blue Creek. It is a good idea for the visiting angler to get a tide table showing tidal movements at the mouth of the river, even if he is fishing as far upstream as Blue Creek, a full thirteen miles or more above the mouth of the river. Fish moving and feeding in the lower twenty miles of the river, as far upstream as Johnson Riffle, will still move and strike a lure or bait on the same timetable as the tides of the ocean.

Blake Hole

Blake Hole and Tarup Riffle just above the hole are two of the finest drift and float fishing areas on the lower Klamath River. This is evidently the first resting spot where both salmon and steelheads hold before moving further upstream on their spawning migrations. New fish move into this area as fish that have been resting here move out, providing a constant and changing number of fresh-run fish.

The action of winter runoffs constantly changes the location of both these spots, but both bank and boat anglers will always find steelies and salmon holding in this area. Even in the late part of the season, salmon will be found resting at Blake Hole. Steelies hold in both the upper end of the hole itself and in the riffle that stretches above and below Tarup mouth.

Bridge Pool

The first steelheads of the season are usually taken by bank or boat fishermen fishing at the old bridge hole, downstream from the highway bridge. The old bridge pool along with the riffles at the mouth of Waukell Creek are prime spots for both trollers working the pool and waders fishing the riffle.

The river here can be fished from both sides, but fly fishing is possible only in the shallower parts of Waukell Riffle. When an angler hooks steelhead or salmon in this part of the river, he meets fish at their very best because they are only a short time out of the ocean. The deep hole at the old bridge is an excellent salmon holding area. Big king salmon can be taken here any time after the first week in July in the average season.

Requa

Most of the boat fishing by trollers is done immediately off the shore at Requa. Anchor lines are not allowed by the Coast Guard, so anglers normally troll in a large circle off this shoreline.

Trolling along the north side of the big islands at the mouth of the river is also popular with salmon fishermen in the tidal basin. Boat docks and launching areas are located all along the lower section of the river from Requa to Terwer Valley. Access to this entire area is excellent.

The Rivers — The Trinity

The Trinity River is what I call a gentleman's stream. By this I mean that it is seldom necessary in fishing the Trinity to wade very deep in order to cast to the steelheads and salmon, nor is it necessary to do a great amount of climbing in order to reach streamside at spots that have good holding or riffle water. In most cases, during the peak seasons, it is possible to drive close to the water.

The type of equipment used to quarter the Trinity River is also pleasantly light for easy fishing. In a few spots, such as in the lower river at Hoopa Valley, it is sometimes necessary to go to long, heavy fly rods and longer spin or casting rods in order to be able to cover the spots where the salmon and steelheads hold. But, for virtually all of my own fishing, I usually am able to use lighter tackle more suited to trout fishing, rather than the big two-fisted rods normally associated with steelhead fishing.

The fact that roads service the Trinity River in most sections of the stream is very important. Only the three gorges of the Trinity are difficult to get to. When trying to locate runs of salmon and steelheads in the Trinity, the angler can fish one

These three steelheads, ranging from a half-pound up to five pounds, illustrate the various sizes this species runs during the fall months. In winter and spring the average steelhead taken from the Trinity will run much larger than these fish.

section to determine whether the fish are on hand and willing to hit. With a few hours drive, he can then move fifty miles or more along the length of the stream to determine whether the fish are in other sections. This is what I call fishing a circuit.

The idea of fishing a circuit hinges on the fact that steelheads or salmon can be in any stretch of the river at any stage of the season. Each angler fishes the river in a slightly different way; although salmon and steelheads may be in a section of the stream, the methods used may not pay off in that section. Often, moving a few miles to another spot will correct this situation.

In my own fishing of the Trinity River, I may even cover most of the length of the stream in a couple of days. In a few cases I can remember, I have started in the early morning hours as far upstream as Lewiston or Douglas City and have ended up at nightfall down on the Hoopa Valley section. I have picked spots along the length of the river that I can drive to directly without much climbing down steep banks. I will fish for a half hour or so in a given stretch and then drive twenty or more miles to another spot where experience has shown that the fish are willing to hit for my own methods of fishing. The entire idea of circuit fishing, or fishing along the length of the stream, is that much of the river can be covered in a short period of time. This makes the Trinity River a special stream for the fisherman.

Trinity River Maps

The maps to the sections of the Trinity River below the two dams in the drainage are mainly concerned with access points and the type of water the angler will find when he reaches the water. This section of the Trinity is primarily salmon and steelhead water. The ability and knowledge needed to get to different sections of the stream, without a great deal of searching on the angler's part, is critical when time is limited. There are many miles of stream involved here; runs of migratory fish can be nearly anywhere in the entire length of the stream.

I have commented only on areas that are readily accessible to the fisherman. In some cases, such as in the Lower Gorge between Hoopa and Weitchpec, I have indicated that it may be necessary for the angler to scale down a rugged cliff in order to gain river access. Anglers in poor health should use caution in steep areas. It is usually possible to find other, nearby areas along the entire length of the river where access is easier.

When utilizing the lower river maps, it is necessary to read the specific sections. All of the roads indicated on the map lead to fishing

A string of steelheads like these on the tailgate of my pickup camper are not particularly hard to come by in Trinity River fishing, providing the angler goes about locating the runs in the right way. The key to Trinity River fishing is to use the extensive road access information in this guide.

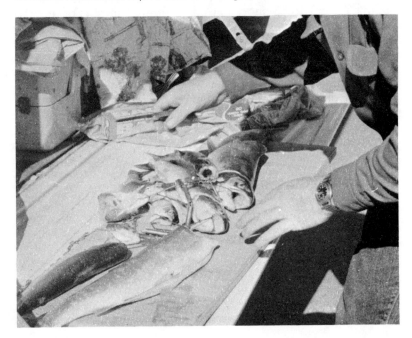

waters and are passable to the average family automobile. Areas and trails with difficult access have, in general, been left off these maps. In some cases, sections of the stream that are hardly worth fishing or that have better fishing waters nearby were left out.

The maps to the upper Trinity River and the major creeks and feeder streams do not include very much access information except where it was deemed necessary to assist the angler in getting to the better fishing spots. Both Coffee Creek and the Upper Trinity River are fine little trout streams, as is the lower section of the East Fork of the Trinity. But access is total, or nearly total, from the roads that parallel the streams here and the angler can usually see the water from these roads.

We have cut off the map of the upper Trinity River at approximately the spot where the Little Trinity River enters the main stream. Except for a short period during the very early season, the stream becomes comparatively small and so do the fish that are taken here.

As a general rule, the closer to the water of Trinity Lake that you fish in these feeder streams the better trout you will take. In fact, on occasion I have found that black bass, particularly the smallmouths, will even enter the feeder streams for a considerable distance when the water temperatures are just right; it can be a lot of fun to take these scrappy little bass from these waters.

Trinity Lake Maps

Trinity Lake is a very fine black bass fishing lake. This is particularly true in the case of smallmouth bass, which prefer rocky underwater areas to those that do not contain rocks or rubble. The Trinity Lake shoreline does not have a lot of rocky areas; this means that at high water, when rocky selections are not visible, the angler after black bass should fish a large segment of the shoreline in order to be certain that he fishes the preferred rocky area. All the shoreline sections of the lake that have large amounts of rocks and rubble have been indicated on the maps. The arrows indicating these rocky sections are as accurate as possible, but at Trinity Lake the rugged shoreline can look all the same at the high-water stages.

While this guide indicates the more productive rocky sections, this does not mean that bass or other game fish will not be found in sections without rocks. Many fish will be taken in areas that have no outstanding features whatever.

Trinity Lake has a relatively limited number of spots where shallow water extends out very far from the shoreline at high water. This makes the few sections that do have underwater shelves even more important to successful fishing. These shelves offer shelter and a ready escape into deep water for both food fish and organisms, as well as for game fish. Bass and other species will be found at the correct temperature level, or as near the correct temperature level as they can find, along these underwater shelves.

Areas where the old river channels were located before dams formed the lakes have been indicated. These areas become important during the warmer period of the year when game fish, particularly trout, seek out the deeper sections of the lake for cooler water. These

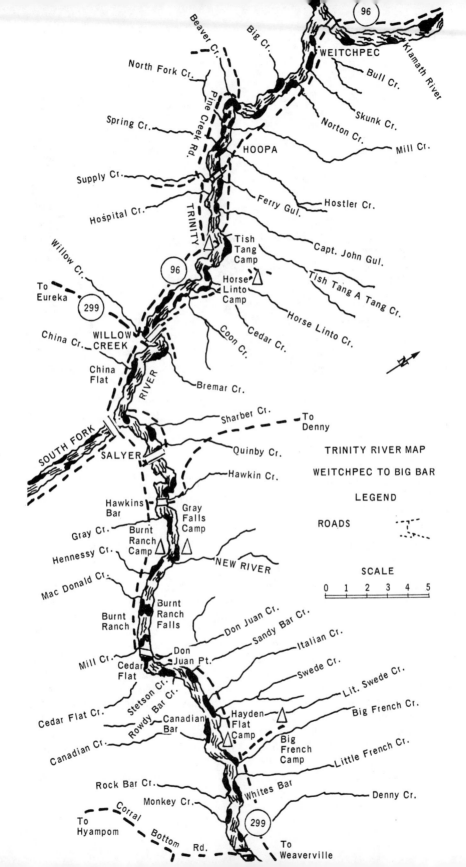

TRINITY RIVER MAP

WEITCHPEC TO BIG BAR

LEGEND

ROADS

SCALE

0 1 2 3 4 5

Although Trinity Lake is mostly known for the quality of the trout fishing, some anglers have discovered that it is also an excellent black bass fishing spot. Not many large bass are found there, however.

areas were located by using official maps from the time before the lakes were formed.

Check Speedometer

It will be necessary for the visiting angler to make an accurate speedometer check in order to use the following information. I have chosen as the speedometer check points the Weitchpec Store and the Mill Creek Bridge at the lower end of the gorge. If you are heading downstream make the first check at the store and if you are heading upstream, or north, make the check at the bridge. Both are readily seen landmarks on Highway 96, the highway that leads from Willow Creek to join with the Klamath River.

Mileages are given from both landmark and speedometer check points.

The Lower Trinity

The small town of Weitchpec sits on the bluff overlooking the point where the Trinity River joins the Klamath River. At this point near the Weitchpec Store, there is the beginning of a seven-mile gorge that is very important for the steelhead and salmon angler during the early season. During the summer months, generally beginning in June, steelheads and salmon move out of the Klamath River and into the deep, protected pools and runs in the first seven miles of river. In the case of the steelies, few fish actually leave these holding pools and runs before the first big rains of the year arrive, usually in the fall.

Fishing in the first gorge can be great during almost any stage of the season; when an angler hits this area at the right time, the fishing can be fantastic. In the past only a few anglers have fished this area because without local advice it is all but impossible for a visitor to locate the several trails that lead down to the water's edge.

Even with the specific information provided in the guide, it will still be necessary for the angler to search for these trails. Some trails are very steep and require a lot of climbing in order to follow them. Others are merely a stroll through the woods. In most cases there is no indication that the trails exist; few of the local people will be willing to lead a visitor to these important access points.

Weitchpec Store

There are access trails that go down the bluff from both ends of the store building. The one on the north side, or Klamath River end, of the store building leads to the mouth of the river and to access to the Klamath River. The road on the south side, or downstream end, of the store building leads down to Weitchpec Falls, a good salmon and steelhead holding pool. The run below the pool is good fly and lure water.

Salmon and steelhead hold in this pool to rest up for the job of go-

These anglers ford the Trinity River in one of the better fly fishing stretches of the first gorge of the Trinity between Hoopa and Weitchpec. Here the river is broad and steelheads or salmon hold in the gorge until after the first rains of the season.

ing over the falls. This is a favorite spot for local anglers. On the north end, the store building is Mile 0; coming from upstream, this would be Mile 7.8 on the speedometer.

Post Office Trail

There are two trails at what is known locally as the Post Office, although there is no post office located at this spot. There is a tiny shack that acts as a marker for the visiting angler. The upstream trail heads past the tiny shack. The second trail heads down the bluff right at a point where a mailbox with the name Smoker is located at the side of the road.

The trail at the mailbox leads to Weitchpec Pool and the lower end of the falls. This trail provides access downstream from the rocky ledge here. The trail by the shack leads to the other side of the falls and provides access to some excellent fly and lure water upstream from the falls. Both of these trails are comparatively easy access points because the highway is not very far above the river here and the land is not as steep as it is in other areas. These access trails are located at Mile .6 from the store and Mile 7.2 from the Mill Creek Bridge.

Deerhorn Road Trail

Deerhorn Road, which connects with Highway 96, marks a little-known access point to the Trinity Gorge. The road is marked. The trail is little more than a stroll through the woods down a relatively mild slope to the river. This access point leads to some really outstanding fly fishing water. The road is at Mile 1.3 from Weitchpec Store and Mile 6.5 from the Mill Creek Bridge. This is one of the easier access points.

Ernie's Road

Ernie Alameda of the Oaks Cafe and Sports in the town of Hoopa has an access road that you can use to drive almost to the river. However, this is private property and you must ask Ernie's permission before using this road. The road has a gate and a key is needed. The access point here to Ernie's Road is at Mile 3.7 from Weitchpec Store and at Mile 4.7 from Mill Creek Bridge.

Norton Creek Trail

Norton Creek Trail leads to some of the best bait and lure fishing water in the first gorge of the Trinity. It is also the steepest of the trails that lead down to the river here. The water is of such high quality, however, that the steep climb is worth the effort for the bait and lure fisherman. Norton Creek Trail is at Mile 3.6 from Weitchpec Store and Mile 4.2 from the Mill Creek Bridge.

Cabin Riffle Trail

At Cabin Riffle Trail fly fisherman will find what is probably the finest fly fishing riffle on the Trinity River. In my own opinion this riffle is one of the finest in the country and worth any effort to get to for the serious fly fisherman. Cabin Riffle provides about three-quarters of a mile of ideal fly water and short casts here will quarter the stream. Cabin Riffle Trail is at Mile 4.7 from Weitchpec Store and Mile 3.1 from Mill Creek Bridge. The trail is steep.

Red Rock Trail

Red Rock Trail leads to the lower end of the gorge, where there is a mixture of lure, bait, and fly water.

A Trinity River steelie like this one, taken from the fall run at Beaver Creek on the Hoopa Indian Reservation, fights as well as or better than any other fish taken in fresh water in the United States. The flow of the river causes some changes in the holding areas, but riffles like Beaver Creek eventually return.

The trail is steep and located at Mile 7.1 from Weitchpec Store and Mile .7 from Mill Creek Bridge.

Beaver Creek Access

Although Beaver Creek Riffle is not in the gorge water, it is such a fine riffle that access .for the fly fisherman is important. From the east bank I have included the location of the primary access road to the riffle on the map. At Beaver Creek Riffle the fly fisherman will find that this is the first point outside of the gorge where steelheads will hold after any sizable rain. The fly fishing conditions are ideal here. The access road that leads to the bar opposite Beaver Creek takes off from Highway 96 at Mile 7.6 from Weitchpec Store and Mile .2 from Mill Creek Bridge. The road has a stop sign on it; follow the road that leads directly to the river. There is a gate on this road that should be kept closed by anglers traveling to and from the river.

Mill Creek

Mill Creek is a sizable creek that has some excellent fly, lure, and bait water near it. The water here is readily visible to the angler, even from the road, so little comment is needed.

The run of water near the mouth of Mill Creek, just north of the town of Hoopa, is one of the best spots on the Trinity River to take fresh-run salmon and steelheads. The best time of year to fish this area is during the fall months of September, October, and November, when the water is cool and clear.

Mill Creek Loop

For many years I have been fishing what I call the Mill Creek Loop. In this fishing I have found that the stretch, from the point where Mill Creek enters the Trinity downstream to the point where the Trinity enters the gorge, is a perfect amount of water for a morning or afternoon of fishing. I then get out of the stream and head back to Mill Creek along the road.

The only problem here is for the angler who does not wade. Some of the best water is located just below Beaver Creek and if the angler does not want to wade he must take the west bank road to the point where Beaver Creek enters the Trinity. To intercept this road, head south on Highway 96 and cross the main road bridge in the town of Hoopa. A short distance south of the bridge there is a church on the west side of the highway. A road, Loop Road (unmarked), heads west. A short distance down the road it connects with Pine Creek. Head downstream until the road heads away from the river. Cross Beaver Creek for access to the excellent riffles and pools below Beaver Creek Riffle.

Pine Creek Road

There are several access roads that lead across the gravel bars to the river. These are plainly visible to anglers driving along Pine Creek Road. The most notable of these roads leads to Deep Sleep Riffle. I have named this riffle for the motel located on the east shore. The riffle is excellent. Deep holes just below and upstream from the motel building almost always have steelheads and salmon in them. You might also want to stay at this motel or talk fishing with its owner, Red Staton. Red is an avid fisherman and always assists visiting anglers who fish the river here. His help is invaluable, especially to the first-time angler on this section of the Trinity.

Post Office Access

There is another access point in the town of Hoopa that actually is Post Office Road. The access road heads down to the river just on the downstream end of the Post Office Building. This road provides access to a series of fine riffles and pools below the main bridge on Highway 96.

Highway Bridge

There is nearly total access to the upstream water of the river from an access road off the east side of the road at the Highway Bridge. You can see the river here and little comment is needed.

Access to the river from the bridge to the upper end of the valley is obvious to any angler traveling Highway 96 and needs no comment other than to say that the river here is, in general, a series of deep holes with shallow riffles in between.

Hoopa Airport Access

There is an access road that leads to the upper end of the valley that takes off from the northern edge of

the Highway Bridge. Follow this road until you see a sign, Airport Road. This road ends on a gravel bar where there are some excellent pools and runs in the upper valley. In general the water downstream and the big hole against the bluff on the far side of the river are the favorite spots in this section. Some fair fly riffles are located upstream, but wading is needed to gain access to this section. At this point, what I call the second gorge of the Trinity begins and there is no public access until Tish Tang Camp.

Tish Tang Camp

Upstream from Hoopa Valley, Highway 96 climbs up and away from the river and access is all but impossible, or through private posted land, except at Tish Tang Forest Service Camp. At Tish Tang you can drive an auto right out onto the gravel bars, where you will find some very fine pools and riffles both up and downstream. There is a regular road system on the bars.

Willow Creek Valley

The next access point is at the spot where the highway again comes down to nearly the level of the river. This road is easy to spot from the road. It leads off across the bar to a series of good fly riffles above Willow Creek airport and some nice holes against the rocky banks. You also gain access to a short stretch of the lower portion of the second Trinity gorge.

Willow Creek

There is an excellent access point at the Willow Creek airport. The access road leads to the south end of

As the sun sets, steelies get restless. This male fish fell for a rapidly moving Spin N Glo lure, even though the water was very roiled. They can sense a fast-moving lure in any kind of water.

the airport strip where there is a big, deep salmon hole that produces salmon every year, especially for local fisherman.

There is also a fine series of riffles right next to the airstrip and downstream from the strip. These riffles are excellent for steelheads and also for runs of shad that enter the river each year in June until the first part of July.

Willow Creek Bridge

There is a bridge crossing the Trinity at Willow Creek. It is reached by turning northeast at River Road in Willow Creek. Anglers wanting to fish the excellent pools and glides of water here can gain access at the north and south

ends of this bridge, called the James McCart Memorial Bridge. The trails are steep and must be used cautiously, but they offer access to some fine water, particularly for the fly fisherman. Both steelheads and shad can be taken here.

Northeast Shore Access

There are two roads on the river bank on the other side of the river from Willow Creek. The road that leads downriver has a single access point a quarter of a mile from where it starts. This access point leads to the opposite side of the airport riffles.

There is no access from the road that leads upriver from the Willow Creek Bridge.

Baseball Field Access

In Willow Creek there is a baseball field. Look for the access road that leads past the southern end of the field to a gravel bar. Here are another series of fine, deep pools and holding areas for salmon, steelheads, and shad.

Twigsville

At Twigsville there is an abandoned lumber mill and mill pond. An access road heads along the south end of the abandoned pond down a steep bank to the river. There is a single, huge salmon hole here and at its deepest part, at a point where the river has dredged out a hole at the base of the rock cliff, salmon can nearly always be found when they are running in this section of the stream.

A smaller hole at the head of this long salmon run is good for either fly fisherman or drift fishing with baits or lures for steelheads. This is a good shad fishing area, although the natives rarely bother to fish here. It is also an excellent area for half-pounders when these fish are running in the fall months.

Downstream from the salmon hole are a series of good riffles that run over a rocky outcropping. These are good for steelheads and, during the runs, shad.

Campbell Ridge Road

The Campbell Ridge Road ends on a gravel bar a half-mile below where the South Fork enters the main Trinity River. This road is reached by taking the bridge at Salyer and the Salyer Loop road to the north. It is doubtful if it is worth taking this extended road because it offers access only to this single gravel bar. The area can be reached from another road on the Highway 299 side just at the point where the highway bridge crosses the South Fork. This road is now blocked off, but the angler can park on the road and walk down past a big blackberry patch to the series of riffles and shallow runs just below the mouth of the South Fork. Steelies and salmon will congregate in this area during the peaks of the migrations; those waiting to go up the South Fork will be found in this area. This section is normally only good after the first heavy rains have raised the water level and cooled the waters of the South Fork.

Salyer Bridge

There is a bridge at Salyer to the northeast side of the river and an access point on the road that heads upriver at Quinby Creek. There are many pools and gliding riffles that are good when runs are in the river. Around the next bend of the river there is another gulch and sandy bar area with access to the same pool and riffle water. In order to fish this area properly, it is normally necessary to cross the stream at a riffle and fish from the Salyer side.

Hawkins Bar Bridge

There is a bridge at Hawkins Bar on the road to Denny. A single access point just across the bridge on the northeast side of the river leads off on the right hand side of the road heading upriver from the bridge. There are some good holding pools where the river has dredged out deep holes at the base of the rocky shoreline.

There is another steep access

trail on the south side of this bridge that leads down just where the bridge touches the south shore. This trail leads to another series of long, deep pools downstream from the bridge.

There is a single access road approximately one mile up the Denny Road. This road is on private property and permission is needed. It is doubtful if this is worth the effort because the road services shallow riffles and pools that have fish in them only when the runs are at peak.

Gray Falls

There is a very steep access road which leads to Gray Falls just south of Gray Falls Camp. This is the active upper limit of runs of shad, which cannot get over considerable falls such as these. The pool below the falls is noted as a tourist attraction as well as a salmon and steelhead holding area. Salmon can be found resting in this pool and those below it nearly any time of the year, but early fall is the time when the biggest concentrations are found here.

Third Trinity Gorge

Above Gray Falls the river is reached only by trail for a few miles up the river to New River. Above this point the river runs through an extremely deep gorge and for nearly eight miles the river is all but inaccessible until Cedar Flat and China Slide.

China Slide

China Slide is a Department of Fish and Game fish stocking point and angling is prohibited 250 feet upstream and downstream at all times. The area outside this restricted area is excellent pool and

riffle water with salmon and steelheads in it any time they are in the river at all. In fact, the fish hole up in this area waiting for fall storms to freshen the water so they can head upstream. Access is rugged.

Cedar Flat

Just upstream from Cedar Flat Resort, there is a bridge to the north side of the Trinity. There is an excellent access point here to a long series of pools and deep riffles that are good fishing. From the bridge to Don Juan Creek are some of the best fishing and holding pools in the shallow canyon section of the Trinity from Cedar Flat to Big Bar.

Sandy Bar

There is steep but good access to deep pools and whitewater riffles in the area between Don Juan Creek and Sandy Bar, especially at Stetson Creek. This entire area features deep holes and short riffles. The road closely parallels the river in this whole stretch from Cedar Flat to Hayden Flat and the angler can see for himself the numerous access points and the type of water that is available. There are deep salmon holes in this entire stretch of water, with some of the best at Hayden Flat, where there is a forest service camp.

Hayden Flat To Big Bar

Between Hayden Flat and Big Bar the access is difficult but possible in nearly every area. The type of water, some deep holding pools with riffles and slow-moving shallow pools, is obvious because the highway closely follows the river. In general, in this area it is best to ford the river and fish the holes and glides from the

This picture shows the Trinity River just below where the North Fork enters. Note the brushy nature of the main Trinity. It can no longer flood and clean out the brushy banks.

south side. This area is normally best after the first few storms of fall, but it is an important stretch because the river is so accessible over nearly its entire length. The steelheads and salmon that come out of the gorge below China Slide will normally make their first rest and pause here. Many fish are taken here each season.

Big Flat

There is some good fly and bait water at Big Flat. Steelheads tend to hold in some of the deeper pools. Only short casts are needed in this section, wading is of little use except to ford the stream in order to work the pools and riffles properly. There is a forest service campground at Big Flat.

Pigeon Point

Some of the better deep pools in this section of the river are located at Pigeon Point on the small bar just upstream from the point. Of the three primary holes, the one formed at the base of the large, round rock on the south shore is usually the most productive for salmon. There is an excellent steelhead riffle at the lower end of the bar; in order to fish it properly, it is necessary to ford the river and fish from the Pigeon Rock or south side at the lower end of the bar.

From the south side the angler can also work a very deep holding pool along the north bank right up against the highway. This hole usually has both salmon and steelheads in it any time the fish are in this part of the river. This pool is best fished with either lures or bait. It is too deep for effective fly fishing.

The five miles of water between Big Flat and Pigeon Point are among the finest holding and pool water on the entire Trinity River upper section. Access is down a steep embankment and the pools and runs can be seen directly from the road, which closely parallels the river here. This access is difficult but not impossible. The best bet in most stages of the water flow is to locate a shallower riffle and ford the stream to fish the river from the south bank. Most of the north bank is steep and very brushy. Both salmon and steelheads will hold in the deeper pools and runs of water between pools at nearly any stage of the runs.

North Fork

A big change in the character of the Trinity River takes place above the mouth of the North Fork. Below this point the river can still flood during the winter runoff periods; this means that in heavy winters the stream has a chance to clean itself of debris and streamside brush any time it floods. Above the mouth of the North Fork and above Canyon Creek, a major tributary, the Trinity becomes very brushy.

It is estimated that nearly a quarter of a million tons of silt are poured into the streambed of the Trinity in the upper stretches of the river above the North Fork by its many tributary streams. The river is dammed at Trinity Dam and Lewiston Dam and can never pour enough water at any stage of the season to sluice off this silt and rubble. The outcome of this complete flow control is the encroachment of very thick stands of brush, reeds, wil-lows, and grasses along the shores of the river and even in the streambed itself. This makes actual access to the water a problem for the angler in the upper river.

Many anglers have taken to rubber rafts and deep wading for long stretches of river in order to continue fishing above the North Fork. Fly fishing is particularly hampered by the thick stands of brush along the shore. In most areas it is all but impossible to get a back cast, except straight up or down stream.

There is a good riffle and deep hole at the mouth of the North Fork. Fish that are going to migrate up the North Fork hold in this deep hole and also in the series of holes and riffles just downstream at Pigeon Point Bar.

Pear Tree Gulch

There are two deep holes and a good series of riffles along the south shore at Pear Tree Gulch. Access to these pools and riffles is across the sandbar on the north shore. The drift fishing technique is the best way to work the holes here.

Elkhorn

There are several deep pools and connecting deep riffles at Elkhorn. There is a very deep salmon hole at Coopers Bar. Just above there is a large dredger bar, across from Red Hill Mine and upstream from Hocker Bar, with a deep salmon hole reached by access across the lower end of the bar.

Junction City

There is an excellent pool and riffle at the Junction City Bridge. Access is a rough road that takes off east from the bridge road on the south side of the river and turns under the bridge. A very rough road leads downstream for a quarter of a mile to a fine salmon pool that nearly always has salmon in it during the runs in this section of the stream. Both bait and lures are effective here.

Between the pool and riffle at the bridge and the deep salmon pool downstream are some fine riffles and deep runs that can be fished by wading down the south bank against the willows and brush.

Soldier Creek Access

By crossing the Junction City Bridge and heading upstream, the angler can reach a good section of the river. The south bank road first heads up and away from the river for 3.5 miles to where it forks through a ranch and heads one mile down the bank to the river. Here it is a good idea to give particular attention to the pool and riffles close to Soldier Creek. This creek pours in cold water during the warm-water months and steelheads and salmon tend to seek these cooler sections, even if they do not like the relative shallowness of the stream here.

There are many rough campsites at Soldier Creek and at the mouth of a spring-fed creek just upstream from Soldier Creek. There is no public access downstream from

A mess of fall-run steelies from the lower sections of the Trinity River. Below the mouth of the North Fork, the Trinity is still able to flood during winter and spring runoffs. Here the stream provides excellent fishing, usually after the first storms of the fall.

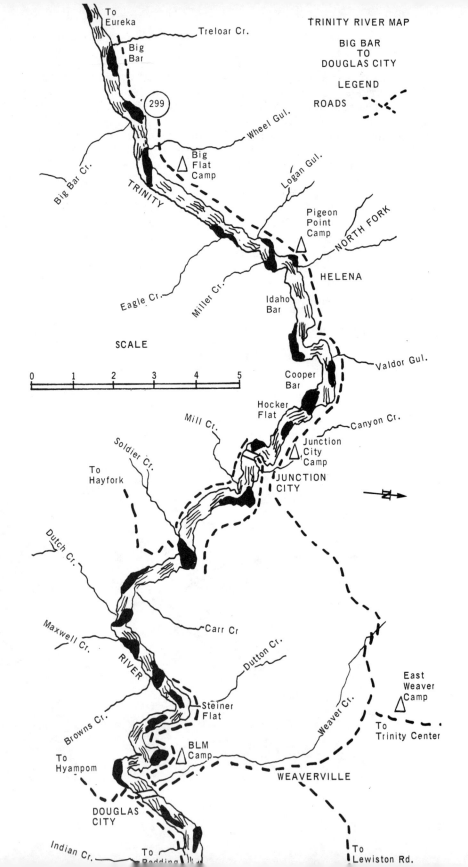

The pool below the bridge at Junction City will normally always have fish in it when they are running in this section of the river. This pool and run of water, along with the water in the next mile or so downstream, is always worth fishing any time after the late summer and early fall runs begin.

the Junction City Bridge nor upstream from the Soldier Creek access.

North Shore Access

Above Junction City there is an access road that heads up river from Highway 299 for approximately three miles. A few hundred yards from where this county road heads upriver, there is an access point across the dredger tailings opposite where Mill Creek enters the river from the south side. This access road leads along the tailings to the river and to a series of shallow pools and riffles upstream. The river is very brushy in most spots. This area does not have any holding water but

is good when runs are moving through this section.

There is an access point approximately one-half mile from the end of this road upstream. The road itself ends on a gravel bar approximately opposite where Soldier Creek enters from the south side. This area, too, features good riffles and shallow slow moving pools. There is no holding water. This entire road is a country road and open to the public, in spite of the fact that landowner posting may be confusing and that certain signs have been changed.

Douglas City

There is an excellent access road at

Douglas City that heads down the north bank of the Trinity River for 4.5 miles. This road also services a large Bureau of Land Management campground that is located just to the west of Douglas City. The road follows the river closely for most of its length. Where the road heads away from the river, there are other access roads along the dredger tailings that line the bank here.

This stretch of the Trinity west of Douglas City offers some of the finest water on the upper river. Huge rocks and rocky areas here have caused very deep holding pools that are used extensively by both salmon and steelheads. You can spot these holes and deep riffles easily from the road.

Right at Douglas City there is a stretch of salmon spawning beds. In the fall the salmon spawn here by the hundreds and steelhead lay in the fast water below the spawning salmon to pick up eggs that float loose from the beds. The area immediately below the bridge at Douglas City is one such area. Other spawning areas can be located in the two-mile stretch of the river above the Douglas City Bridge.

Union Hill Road

There is an old mining access road that heads up the Trinity River along the north bank that services a relatively remote area of the stream seldom fished by other than local people. This road is fairly difficult to locate for the first-time fisherman. The road takes off east from Highway 299 at a point along the road between Weaverville and Douglas City right where the highway crosses Weaver Creek from Douglas City. The road isn't marked in any way, but it is the only road heading east

from Highway 299 at this spot. The road is very steep in most spots but is passable for the passenger car.

To get to the river, stay to the left on all roads except for a single road at the summit that is marked as private property.

The road ends at a meadow on the river's north side. There are good fly riffles about every quarter of a mile in this area and just where the road contacts the river there is a huge hole formed by the abutment of an old bridge. This was once called Iron Bridge. All the land along this road is under Bureau of Land Management and not posted. There is a trail leading upriver to another series of pools and riffles.

Iron Bridge Road

About 2.5 miles above the Douglas City Bridge is Iron Bridge access road. For the first mile or so you will find a great deal of posted property, but near the end of the road the land is owned by Bureau of Land Management and is open to the public. This road services the south side of the river from the same area as Union Hill Road. The road ends at a good Bureau of Land Management rough campground that has tables and fireplaces. It is one of the better campsites in this section of the Trinity. The road is passable to any type of vehicle. This area is rarely fished by visiting anglers.

Poker Bar Access

There is an access road at Poker Bar Road that leads to the Reo Stott real estate holding. Stott has put in a pair of bridges to the north side of the river to provide access for the people who have purchased property here. The public is allowed access to

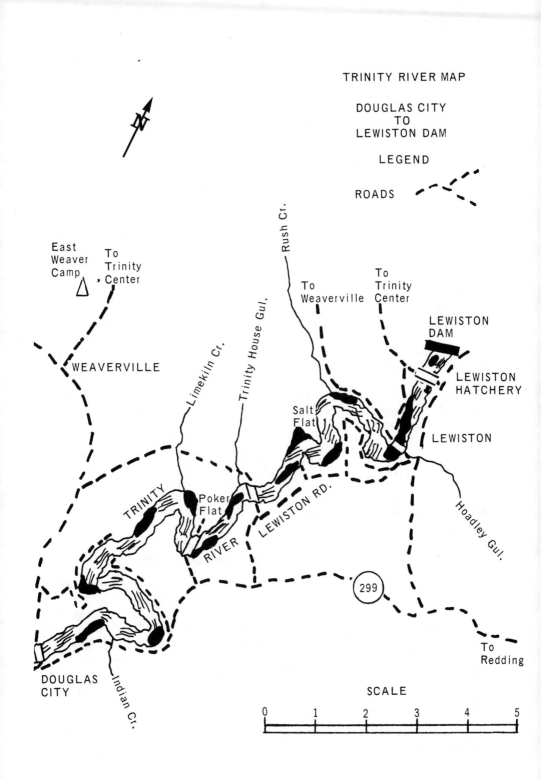

TRINITY RIVER MAP

DOUGLAS CITY
TO
LEWISTON DAM

LEGEND

ROADS

East
Weaver
Camp

To
Trinity
Center

To
Weaverville

To
Trinity
Center

LEWISTON
DAM

WEAVERVILLE

Rush Cr.

LEWISTON
HATCHERY

Limekiln Cr.

Trinity House Gul.

Salt
Flat

LEWISTON

TRINITY

Poker
Flat

LEWISTON RD.

Hoadley Gul.

RIVER

299

DOUGLAS
CITY

Indian Cr.

To
Redding

SCALE

0   1   2   3   4   5

the river here, even though it is private property, providing anglers ask and obtain permission from the people at Poker Bar Lodge. Anglers who do not seek permission will be denied the right to fish.

The Poker Bar area is among the better spots to fish in this section of the river. The water here is a series of relatively shallow pools interspersed with sections of whitewater riffles. Fly fishing can be excellent when there is a run of steelheads in the area.

Bucktail Access

By taking the old Lewiston Road turnoff, you can gain access to the river at Bucktail Road from the north side of the river. Here the access is limited to the area around the bridge. This section is deeper than most, however, and will hold quite a few salmon or steelheads nearly any time that the fish are running.

Goose Ranch Road

There is a good access road that takes off from the old Lewiston Road and heads along the river for a little over 2.3 miles ending in the town of Lewiston at Viola Road. This road has a lot of posted private property, but there are several access points not posted that head down across the dredger tailings. Most of this area is slow moving and rather shallow pool water, but there are several good riffles that will give up steelheads when they are in the area.

Old Bridge Access

There are two very short access roads at the old bridge on the south end of Lewiston. The old bridge is the starting point for the special fly-fishing-only section of the upper Trinity. This area is noted for the number of large brown trout that it gives up to fly fishermen each season. Another access point is found on the east side of the river at the old bridge.

New Bridge Access

There are two roads, one on each side of the Trinity Dam Road on the east side of the river. These two short roads lead to the streamside right at the new bridge and feature some of the deepest pools in the upper river. No fishing is allowed 250 feet from the fish ladder at the small dam just above the new bridge.

Lewiston Hatchery Access

There are several access points down the road that leads from the Trinity Dam Road to the Lewiston Hatchery, a distance of approximately one mile. This is almost all riffle water that is ideal for fly fishing. Each season many large brown trout are taken from this stretch as well as the stretch between the two bridges at Lewiston.

Access Roads to South Fork

Access is very limited to the lower South Fork of the Trinity River. In fact, most of the access is not good. However, often the South Fork can provide excellent fishing if the angler manages to hit it at the right stage of the season. In some sections that can be reached with the average automobile, there are good holding pools that are worth fishing. In general, the South Fork does not carry a great deal of water and salmon or steelheads will seldom be found in the shallow sections of the stream. Rather, the fish moving through this area will usually be found in the deeper waters of the steep canyon of the South Fork.

Lower South Fork

An access road takes off from Highway 299 just a short distance upstream from the mouth of the South Fork just above Salyer. This road mostly runs along the ridge, but 6.3 miles along its course there is a short access road to some very fine, deep pools that hold salmon or steelheads when the fish are migrating in this section of the stream. At this access point there are several good rough campsites. Access is down the steep bank to the water.

Another access road is located 2.2 miles from a forest service sign on the east bank road that says Surprise Creek and South Fork Trail. Here you will find more deep holding pools that hold fish any time they are in this section of the South Fork. There are also some shallow holes in this area and some deep, gliding riffles that are fair to good for fly and lure fishing.

Trinity River — South Fork

There is limited access to the South Fork of the Trinity in Hyampom Valley. In the valley itself the South Fork runs through a broad flood plain. In the 1964 flood the river scoured itself a great deal. What remains of the streambed is made up primarily of small gravel and small rock beds. This stretch of river has no holding water for either salmon or steelheads.

The best places to fish here are where logs and occasional large boulders have settled in the stream bed. Where these obstructions are found, the river has gouged out fairly deep pools and holds whatever salmon or steelheads are on hand.

Bridge

A bridge spans the South Fork at the south end of Hyampom Valley and a short access road on the west bank leads to some fairly deep holes and runs of water about a half-mile above the bridge itself. These huge boulders and the run of water for the next few miles upstream in the South Fork are salmon and steelhead holding pools and are among the best spots to fish in this area.

South Fork Access

Access to the South Fork downstream from the bridge at the south end of the valley to the lower end of the valley is down a series of crude roads or trails over a sandbar. These roads are made new each year by anglers fishing the stream and are readily visible from the paved road on the west bank and the rough road that leads north out of Hyampom.

Big Slide Camp

At Big Slide Campground the river changes character from the flat flood plain to deep pocket and pool water where it passes through a very deep, rocky canyon. The rocks and boulders have caused deep holes; these begin just downstream from Big Slide Campground. Any salmon or steelheads in the South Fork will hold in these very deep holes, deep riffles, and short stretches of riffle water.

Monroe Creek

A half mile downstream from Big

Slide Camp is Monroe Creek. This creek carries a good head of water year around during most years. It provides a supply of cool water that tends to hold salmon and steelheads in the deep holes and runs just near the mouth and downstream from the mouth of Monroe Creek. This area can be reached from the creek mouth itself or by way of Big Slide Camp.

Manzanita Ranch

Seven miles downstream from Big Slide Camp, there is an access point at Manzanita Ranch. A power line crosses the gorge of the South Fork at this point and there is a large parking area directly under the power lines. Access is down a steep, rocky cliff to some good pool water at this spot. This is all holding water in this section.

Glen Forest

Highway 3 and Highway 36 lead to Glen Forest, the only other section of the South Fork that is accessible to the fisherman. The bridge at Glen Forest marks the upper limits of legal winter fishing on the South Fork. There are some excellent deep pools downstream from the bridge that hold salmon nearly all year and steelheads when they are running in this area.

Lumber Road Access

Highway 36 climbs up and away from the South Fork after it crosses to the west bank. Access is impossible in this area except for a few forest service roads that lead down to the river. There is a lot of lumbering activity here and more roads may provide access in the future.

In this section of the South Fork, you will find primarily deep pools and deep riffles interspersed with white water. The river runs through a very rugged, steep, and rocky gorge. Salmon and steelheads find holding pools in this entire area. Access is the primary problem and even that which is available is very rugged.

Lewiston Lake

Lewiston Lake is one of the finest trout fishing lakes in the entire west. The growth factor for the trout planted here is truly amazing. Trout planted at eight or nine inches will reach fourteen inches and will weigh over a pound within a single season. Many specimens of rainbow and brown trout at Lewiston will go well over the five-pound mark.

At Lewiston Lake the main thing that makes for good trout fishing is the fact that the water drained out of Trinity Dam and Clair Engle Lake is taken from deep within the upper lake. This means that the water flowing into Lewiston is always very cold. Unlike most lakes that have standing water, the water in Lewiston Lake is constantly drained out and sent through a tunnel to furnish water to Whiskeytown Lake and the Sacramento River. This continual flushing action keeps the water homogenized—the mixing action provides perfect temperatures and habitat for trout.

Lewiston Lake is not an extremely deep body of water. Fishing is the primary water sport at the lake and fast boating and water skiing are not allowed. The angler can use virtually any type of fishing equipment to take trout from Lewiston.

In the spring the fishing at Lewiston Lake can be fast and furious. These anglers show how it's done in some shoreline action between Lewiston Lake and the base of Trinity Dam.

Lewiston Lake is the reregulating reservoir below Trinity Dam and the diversion point for transporting Trinity River water to Whiskeytown Reservoir. Lewiston has about fifteen miles of shoreline and 610 surface acres of water.

The Department of Fish and Game has stocked catchable-sized fingerling rainbow trout. In addition to the stocked fish, there is a considerable recruitment of fish from Trinity Lake through both the spillway and the powerhouse.

Fly Fishing

At Lewiston Lake the fortunate combination of clear and cold water makes for excellent fly fishing. The trout do not go too deep in the lake and casting or trolling flies is one of the best ways to take them. There are several areas along the west shore where even shallow wading will get the flycaster into good trout fishing areas.

One of the premium areas for fly fishing is in the short section of the Trinity River between the base of Trinity Dam and the main body of Lewiston Lake. Here, off-and-on power-making activity at Trinity Dam causes masses of food to be sucked up by the outflowing cold water and deposited in Lewiston. Generally, early in the morning power making is at a minimum and this part of the lake, just below the dam, is a standing body of water. But when the generators are turned on and water begins to flow into

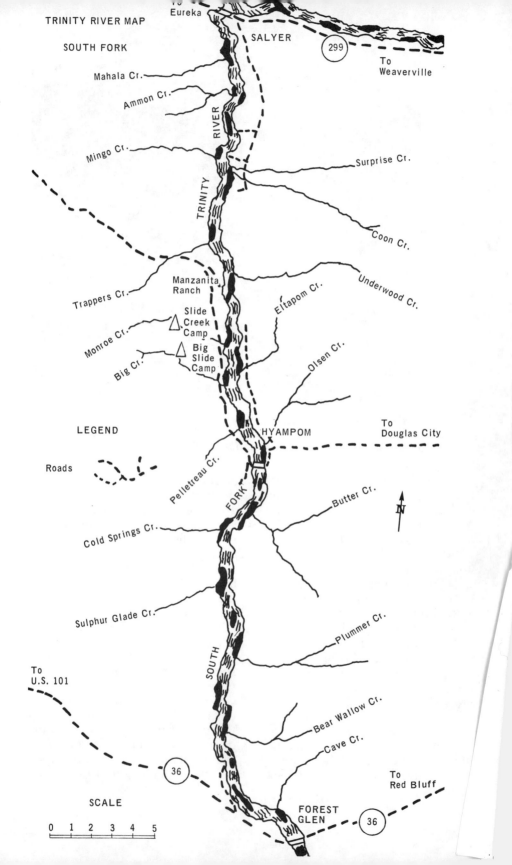

TRINITY RIVER MAP

SOUTH FORK

To Eureka

SALYER

To Weaverville

Mahala Cr.

Ammon Cr.

TRINITY RIVER

Mingo Cr.

Surprise Cr.

Coon Cr.

Underwood Cr.

Manzanita Ranch

Trappers Cr.

Eltapom Cr.

Slide Creek Camp

Monroe Cr.

Olsen Cr.

Big Slide Camp

Big Cr.

LEGEND

To Douglas City

HYAMPOM

Roads

Pelletreau Cr.

SOUTH FORK

Butter Cr.

N

Cold Springs Cr.

Sulphur Glade Cr.

Plummer Cr.

To U.S. 101

SOUTH

Bear Wallow Cr.

Cave Cr.

To Red Bluff

FOREST GLEN

SCALE

0 1 2 3 4 5

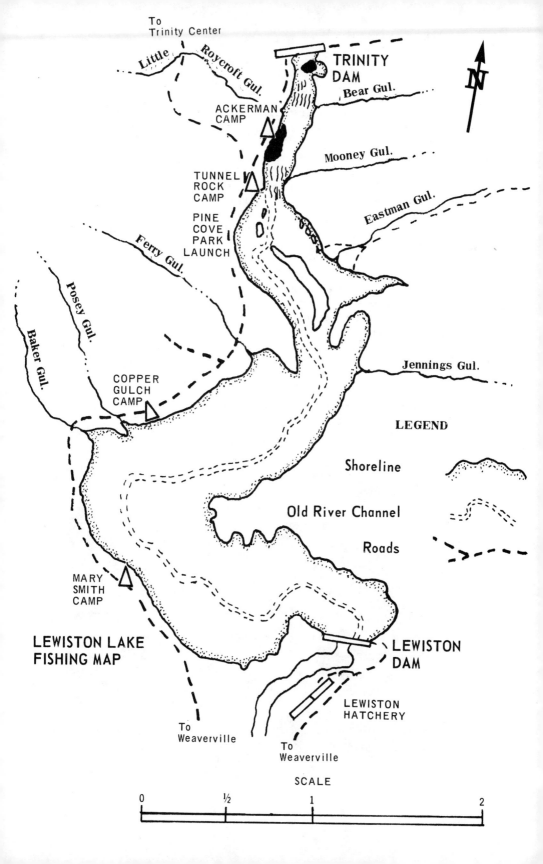

Lewiston, the trout in this section go on a feeding binge.

When the water is still you can actually see large trout milling around in a random pattern in the neck of water between the two lakes. But when the generators start to discharge water, all of the trout will instantly turn into the current and begin feeding. It generally takes about an hour after the start of power making before the trout stop feeding. Also, after about half an hour, moss begins to flow down with the current and it becomes difficult to fish without picking up a lot of this green moss. But for the first half hour to hour of power making, fishing can be fantastic.

The way I generally fish this upper section of Lewiston is to take the boat fairly close to the dam just before power making begins. I do not set an anchor. Rather, I allow the boat to drift with the current about midway from one bank to the other. I then cast in toward the shoreline and retrieve back to the boat.

Heavily weighted flies are not needed for this kind of fishing because the boat is moving along at about the same speed as the sinking or floating fly and there is little or no resistance from the current. In most cases, I have had my best luck fishing the east shoreline along the rocky bank against the dredger tailings where the trout find protection from the considerable current at peak power-making activities. Of particular interest in this area is the cold spring water flowing into the

The results of a few hours of fishing at Lewiston Lake. This lake is one of the finest trout fishing lakes in California. The trout fishing conditions are kept good during the season by cool Trinity Lake water flowing into Lewiston.

This rainbow is a bit better than the average trout that is taken at Lewiston, but fish like these are by no means an exception. For the fly fisherman, it can be a supreme challenge to take trout in the reeds and brushy sections of the lake.

lake about halfway between the dam and Pine Cove Park. The trout hold out in front of this spring creek by the hundreds. You can see them in the deeper cuts in the lake bottom here and in the mouth of the spring itself. I have taken many limits of trout from this area.

Fly fishing is excellent around the islands out in front of the Pine Cove Park docks. Here I idle the motor of my boat slowly and fish in toward the shoreline of the dredger tailings. Early mornings and late evenings are the best times to fish. Later in the day the trout go deeper. The channel to the east of these islands is excellent for dry fly fishing because even in a fairly heavy wind this area remains calm enough so that you can work dry flies with high floating fly lines.

The area of willows just past where the main lake is formed is an exceptional fly fishing spot. Here I have found that it is best to wait until the sun has had a chance to warm the water slightly. The warming action of the sun triggers a hatch of mayflies and other aquatic insects, usually around ten to twelve in the morning and again just before sunset. Large trout move out of the main body of the lake and cruise in among the drowned willows. The best way to take these trout is to cast, allow a nymph pattern to sink almost to the bottom, and then retrieve very slowly to the surface. I usually tie up to the brush for this fishing if the wind is blowing because it is difficult to get a fly to sink deep enough when the wind is moving the boat. When

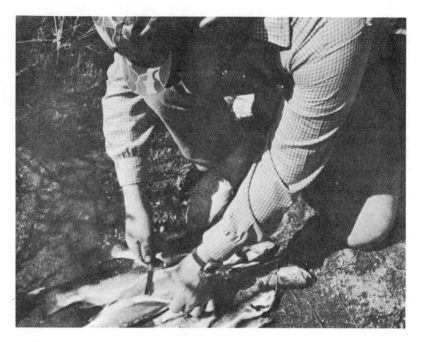

Author cleans the day's catch and carefully checks stomach contents. By noting what the trout have been eating, it is possible to narrow down the choice of baits that should be offered and to choose with intelligence what the trout want on their menu. These trout had a little of everything in them.

the wind is only blowing slightly or when it is dead calm, I prefer to let the boat drift over the openings in the brush.

In this area also, you can fish the shallow, weedy areas with a fly that is barely under the surface. The trout that come into this area are actively feeding and they are relatively willing to take a fly. You can see them cruising; the trick is to estimate which direction they are going to go and then to cast well in front of them. If you cast directly to the cruising trout, he will nearly always spook. The best time to fish the very shallow areas here is early or late in the day when the light is subdued. In the sunlight the larger trout rarely will be found in this shallow water.

Along the west shore just north of Pine Cove are several shallow shelves that can be waded by shore fishermen. Here the best bet is to fish early and late. Trout cruise this shoreline virtually all day long and these points of land jutting out close to the channel of the old river bed are excellent access points to the dropoff into deeper water.

Trolling Lewiston Lake

The majority of the trolling done at Lewiston Lake is done in the northern half of the lake. The area just off the Pine Cove docks is popular, as is the channel area below this point near the islands. It is not necessary to troll very deep in this area but at all times of the year, except early spring and again in October, it is generally necessary to troll early and late in the day.

In the main body of the lake, the best bet for the troller is to troll in the areas charted on the map as the old stream bed. In general, the trout will be in these deep channels, or very near them, for the bulk of the season and during the warmer parts of the day. The troller can add some weight to his trolling rig here and fish deep for larger fish.

Early and late in the day trout will move inshore in order to feed along both the east and west shorelines. Trolling about forty to sixty feet from shore is then a good method. Some anglers insist on using flashers for fishing Lewiston lake, but I do just as well trolling spoons and lures like the Rebel, Rapala, or Flatfish. When trolling without flasher blades, it is possible to get relatively deep to fish the main body of the lake with the addition of very little extra weight. With the flasher rigs, you have to use a lot of weight or wire lines and extremely heavy tackle is then needed in order to handle the heavy lines and weights. I generally only use spinning lines of 4-pound test or lighter for fishing Lewiston Lake.

Lures for Lewiston

Most anglers who fish Lewiston Lake troll or fish with bait from shore, but I've found that I can do just as well or better by casting with lures of almost any kind. I allow the

One of the best weight limits the author has ever taken from Lewiston Lake. There are two times of year, spring and fall, when this kind of string of trout can be expected. Even in the summer the cool waters of the lake can produce excellent limits of trout.

boat to drift with the current or in the wind and repeatedly cast to one side of the boat then the other. By counting, you can determine how deep a sinking lure is going and once you locate a single fish there is a pretty good chance that others are in the same area.

By casting this way instead of trolling, it is possible to cover a wide swath of water at a variety of depths in order to locate the trout. Trolling only covers one single line and only one single depth on each pass. I use metal spoons for most of my own Lewiston Lake lure fishing because they cast well, need no extra weights or special rigging, and because they take as many trout as other lures. However, I've had some good days fishing with Rebel type lures, Lazy Ike and Flatfish trolling, and even slow trolling the larger metal spoons. With lures, the fish you do take are generally the larger specimens.

Bait Fishing

There is very little the angler can do at Lewiston Lake in the way of collecting natural baits out of the water. The only place at all where aquatic insects are available is just below Trinity Dam; this is very dangerous because the flow of water can be altered in a very short time. But all of the common baits—such as roe, garden worms, nightcrawlers, and marshmallows—are used.

The shore fisherman will do best if he moves his baits frequently. It is also a good idea for the bait fisherman to move from place to place if he isn't taking trout regularly. I would say that if the angler hasn't taken a trout while bait fishing within half an hour, it is time to move to another spot. When fishing from a boat, it is often better to let the boat drift and move the bait along the bottom. This offers the bait to many times more fish than would be the case if the angler fished in one spot.

Trinity Lake

Although Trinity Lake is noted for the high quality of the trout fishing to be found, there is also a considerable amount of black bass fishing for both smallmouths and largemouths. The smallmouths are more numerous than the largemouths in a lake such as Trinity (Clair Engle) Lake because there is not a great deal of the brushy cover preferred by largemouths.

In general, the smallmouths will be found in the rocky areas and the largemouths will be found at or around the many sunken stumps that dot the shoreline of the lake. This does not mean that these fish will only be found in these areas, rather, they will be more numerous where these features are found than in areas devoid of cover.

Except in a few spots, the Trinity shorelines are not what could be called rocky areas. On points of land that jut out from the lake and exposed to heavy pounding from the winds, there are what I call developing rocky areas. These developing rocky areas are formed when wind and wave action erode the dirt and silt from the rock formations. As the years go by, these areas become more pronounced rocky formations that cascade down under the current level of the lake surface.

Trinity Lake Trout

When Trinity Lake was first filled, the trout fishing was an amazing

*At Trinity Lake the angler can take trout at all stages of the
season, but during each season he must change his tactics in
order to be sure he is fishing at the right depth.*

thing to behold. As the water began
to rise behind the dam, it covered
acres of extremely fertile slopes and
the food supply for the fish planted
at the lake was outstanding. This
meant that the trout planted in the
lake had what amounted to an endless supply of food, and they grew at
a very rapid rate during the first few
years.

However, after the first four
years, the trout fishing began to
taper off at a rapid rate. The reason
for this is that food for fish can only
be produced down the slopes of the
lake as far as the sun's light can
penetrate. At Trinity the basic
shoreline is extremely steep and
this means that the food-producing
zones are relatively limited compared with the volume of water con-
tained in the lake. This limits the

food supply.

The decline of fishing quality
was steady at Trinity Lake all during
the 60s until it bottomed out around
1967. Then the vast number of fish
that were produced during the ex-
plosion of population and growth
during the early years of the lake's
existence had leveled off to the point
where food production, fish growth,
and survival had also leveled off.
Today, Trinity Lake is what I call a
stabilized body of water. The trout
fishing, for those who go about it
right, provides good, high-quality
sport.

The basics of Trinity Lake trout
fishing are about the same as for
fishing any other body of medium
altitude water. The trout follow a
definite pattern and at given seasons
they will be found in certain areas.

Trinity Lake is noted for the high quality of the trout fishing to be found there. Fine rainbows like this one have found perfect conditions now that the lake has settled down and the production of food and fish has stabilized.

Spring

In the spring the rainbow trout at Trinity will generally be found in or very near to the feeder streams of the lake. Before the opening of the general trout fishing season, the angler should fish as near to these feeder streams as he can get because there is a regular commuter traffic of rainbows going to and returning from the spawning beds of any of the tributary streams that feed into the lake.

The brown trout also gather near these same tributaries because they find a constant supply of food being washed into the lake by the tributaries. Their favorite diet of small fish migrating into the lake comes down from these streams. However, brown trout will also be found roaming along the general shoreline even in areas where there are no sizable tributary streams.

Summer

In the early summer, before the surface temperatures of the lake begin to warm, the rainbows will begin to move all over the lake. I have found that it is best to fish the sections where deep, old river channels run close to areas with large shallow, food-laden masses of land that protrude out into the lake. Rainbows and browns will congregate in areas such as this because it is possible for them to move up onto the shallow areas to feed and then retreat during the daylight hours into the deeper areas such as the old river channels.

Virtually every feeder stream into the lake has these shallow areas, but those found in the major streams are generally much larger and hold many more trout. The Stuart Fork, East Fork of Stuart Fork, Swift Creek, Main Trinity, and East Fork of the Trinity arms of the lake all will have good populations of trout at this time of the year because they have large areas of shallow water located near deep water.

If the angler will check out areas such as the dredger tailings at the far north end of the lake, he will see that there are almost endless numbers of minnows, nymphs, and other food forms that seek out the protection of the dredger rock piles. The trout move into this area when hatches of insects occur and they lurk just outside of the rocky areas and the general shallow waters, waiting for the inshore minnows to make a mistake.

In late summer trout seek the cool water at Trinity Lake. However, I have checked the depths at which trout range during the period from about mid-July through mid-September and have seldom found them holding in water more than thirty to forty feet in depth. Trinity

The author examines the stomach contents of a Trinity Lake trout. For several years Trinity Lake trout suffered from a lack of food. Since then the feed in the lake has stabilized at a high level and all the trout have a good food supply.

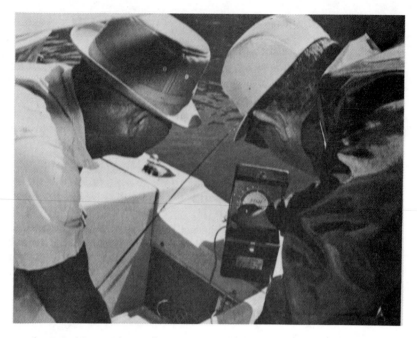

Author working with a Fish Lo Kator to find underwater shelves that are so important to successful lake fishing for both black bass and trout. When you know the location of these drowned shelves of land sticking out in the lake, you've found the fish's dining room table.

Lake is a relatively cool body of water and the trout can generally find the proper 55 to 70 degree water that they prefer at relatively shallow depths. The location of the old river channels is important in areas near the feeder streams, but it becomes less important to successful trolling or drift fishing the closer to the dam the angler fishes.

Trinity Trout Fishing

From the above seasonal outline, the reader will see, by the continual reference to the trout traffic in the general areas of the feeder streams, that this area of the lake is very important. The reason for this is that Trinity Lake is formed in exceptionally steep canyons, when compared with most lakes. Any time that the shorelines are steep, the food zone along the bank is extremely limited. Trout just naturally move toward areas where they find a combination of the proper temperatures and a ready supply of food. Therefore, the best areas to fish at Trinity are those that are near the feeder streams and contain substantial amounts of fairly shallow water. These are clearly marked on the map in this guide.

Of course, limits of trout can be taken in areas other than at or near these feeder streams. There is so much water to be explored in a big, deep lake like Trinity that the average angler is better off fishing these relatively compact zones of the food rich areas rather than the general lake waters. If the angler has an electronic fish locating device, such as the Fish Lo Kator that I use, he can effectively locate concentrations of trout or kokanee fairly easily in areas other than near the feeder streams and the dropoffs into deeper water in these zones. But if the angler does not have the use of one of these electronic devices, he will have to be ready to spend a good deal of time in order to locate the concentrations of trout in the general lake.

Trout Trolling

The fact that trout at Trinity Lake seldom go into water of more than fifty feet in depth makes trolling an effective method of taking trout.

With an outfit fitted with 6- to 10-pound test monofilament, the angler can normally get down to fishing depths for trout with only a few ounces of weight. With line that tests even less, down to two or four pounds breaking strength, the angler can often get down to the proper depths with only a couple of ounces of weight.

When attempting to locate the correct depths, a troller should utilize every factor until he gets the right formula for any specific day of fishing. If there is more than one rod in the boat when trolling, each angler should try to fish at a different depth. For instance, if one angler is using a two-ounce weight, the other should use perhaps four

Some of the author's favorite lures for trolling in lakes like the Trinity, and for general trout fishing in California. From this selection, the angler should be able to choose a few lures that will produce almost any time during the year. In warm water, weight must be added to take lures down.

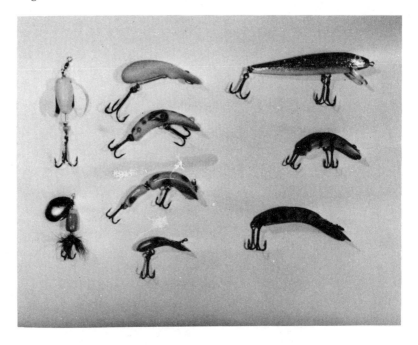

ounces of weight. Also, as a general rule, if you do not take fish within a reasonable period of time—perhaps a half hour of trolling—it is generally best to add more weight for the next half hour of fishing. Continue to add weight and go deeper until the proper formula is found. Once the proper depth, rolling speed, and lure or bait combination is found, it is easy to take a limit of Trinity Lake trout. But until this combination is found, the angler will not do very well.

Drift Fishing

Drift fishing with bait is a very effective method of taking Trinity Lake trout. The simplest way to fish at the proper depth is to rig with the weight on the end of the line and the bait on a dropper strand from three to five feet up the line from the weight. The line is let out until the weight touches the bottom and then lifted a foot or so up from the bottom. This keeps the bait in the proper zone of the water, within ten feet of the bottom. By repeatedly dropping the weight down to the bottom, the angler can be certain that he is working the bait in this correct zone.

The main thing for the angler to watch for in drift fishing is that he fish in water of the proper depth and in areas where the proper temperatures are at hand. If the angler finds that he has drifted into an area that is much more than fifty feet deep, or into one where the water temperatures are above or below 55 to 68 degrees, he should pick up and move to another area that has these

The Rebel lure, probably more used than any other by Trinity Lake regulars, is an excellent choice for the trout or bass fisherman. Often an angler can even troll with no additional weight and still take both species by working along the shorelines of the lake.

elements. Trout will simply not stay for long in any area that does not have the proper temperature and the proper depths.

Temperature

Temperature, more than any other single element, controls the movements and lives of fish, trout included. A simple, inexpensive water thermometer can be used by the angler in order to determine if he is fishing in areas that have the proper temperature for the species he is fishing for.

The temperatures preferred by the fish found in Trinity Lake are 55 to 65 degrees for rainbows, brown, brook, and landlocked steelhead trout. For largemouth bass, 68 to 72 degrees is ideal and for smallmouth bass, 62 to 72 degrees is right. Panfish generally prefer water of 65 to 72 degrees. At these temperatures, each species is most active. If an angler cannot find the exact temperature preference level for the species he is fishing for, he should look for temperatures as near to these ideal temperatures as possible.

The Depth-O-Plug thermometer indicates the temperatures and the depths to which it has sunk. The normal way of using the thermometer is to connect it to the fishing line with a simple snap swivel and then cast it out or drop it straight down into the water. Allow the thermometer to remain at a given depth for a reasonable period of time and then reel it in rapidly so that the change in reading is fairly small. The water level in the barrel will indicate just how deep the thermometer sank on the cast.

The ideal situation is to locate the proper temperature for a certain species where there is also bottom. Species such as black bass will nearly always be found right on or very near the bottom. Even trout, which roam a good deal more than bass, will usually be found fairly close to the bottom, providing they can find the proper temperature ridges and slopes to navigate from the feeding areas in fairly shallow water and to return to the deeper sanctuary waters where they rest between feeding periods. This is another reason why the underwater contour of the lake is so important to successful fishing at Trinity Lake or any other body of water.

I have found in fishing Trinity Lake that most species of fish prefer slightly cooler water than in many lakes in California. Trinity is a relatively cool body of water and the periods when the water levels are down are extended. I feel that this causes Trinity Lake fish to prefer cooler water by as much as 3 to 5 degrees less than in many lakes, such as Shasta and Berryessa, where I did extensive temperature checks.

The importance of making temperature checks from time to time in Trinity Lake fishing is pointed up by the fact that, even during the hot summer months, wind action in many of the arms of the lake can cause the temperature of certain areas to be as much as 8 to 10 degrees warmer or cooler than other spots, while the general temperature is far different from one spot to another. For instance, if the wind is blowing from west to east, the water in the arms of the lake like Stuart Fork or the Papoose Creek arms can be very different in the premium upper levels than it is in areas like the East Fork of the Stuart Fork. These changes in temperature due to wind and wave action can be

Pat Freeman displays an average Trinity Lake black bass. Although the bass do get a good deal bigger than this in many cases, particularly when taken from deeper water with jigs and plastic worms, most of the bass the angler will see still range from one to two and a half pounds.

all-important to a day of fishing. The only way to certain that you are fishing in areas with the proper temperature for the species involved is to actually take temperature checks from time to time.

I use two thermometers in my own fishing. One thermometer is attached directly to the fish stringer and put over the side as soon as I begin to fish. This gives me a constant check on the surface temperature. Through the years I have found that at certain temperatures the surface waters will provide good fishing using certain methods with my own equipment.

The second thermometer is used when I enter a new area of the lake. I cast this thermometer out and allow it to settle to the bottom.

It gives me not only a check on the bottom temperature in this new area, but also indicates how deep this particular area is without using the Fish Lo Kator.

Underwater Ridges

On the Trinity Lake map in this guide, I have indicated rocky areas, along with developing rocky areas, even when the amount of rubble is relatively small, because Trinity Lake doesn't have a lot of choice sections. More important to the serious black bass fisherman, I have indicated sections of the lake that have underwater ridges or outcroppings of land that protrude from the shoreline. These are not readily seen by anglers fishing during high-water periods of the year, although anglers fishing here during the fall months can see these areas with no trouble.

The information about these underwater outcroppings was gathered by using Geological Survey maps of the area before the lake was ever built; by utilizing a fish locator sonar device; and by personal observation at high, medium, and low stages of the water level at Trinity Lake. The areas are indicated on the map as a tone of dots and are as accurate as feasible for the fisherman's purposes.

An angler who is fishing for black bass of any type will do better to concentrate his efforts in areas that feature a lot of underwater structure, as shown on the maps. Bass are very serious about the type of habitat and the depths at which they will hold. Trinity Lake stratifies during the warm-water periods and bass can be found only at certain depths at a given time of the season. By fishing areas with a lot of underwater structure, the angler has a much wider band of bottom at a given depth.

Trinity Shoreline

In general the shoreline at Trinity Lake is extremely steep. This means that in areas where it is steep the zone or depth where the bass will be found will be very narrow and extreme accuracy is needed to take bass. Because there are only a relatively few areas with gently sloping shorelines, the following maps are especially effective.

This is what it's all about. A good fish is taken trolling near the top at Trinity Lake. As a bonus, the lake lays in some of the most inspiring scenery in the entire state.

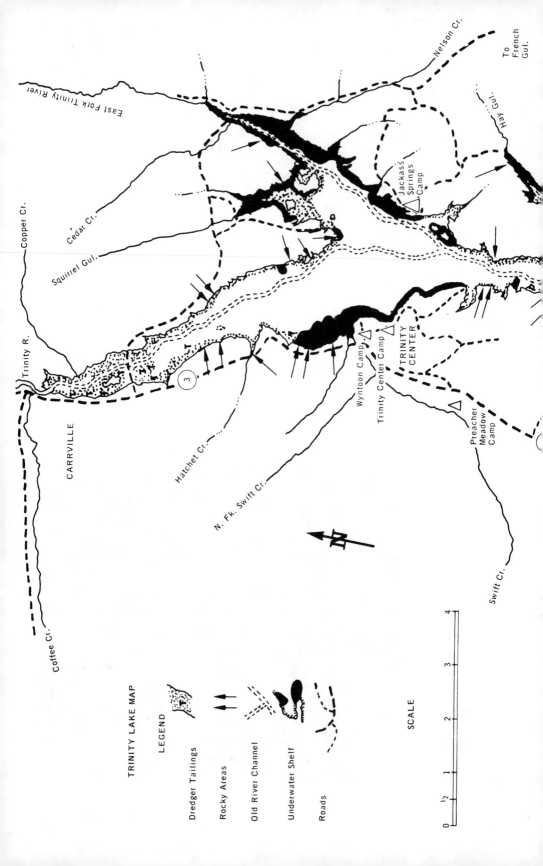

TRINITY LAKE MAP

LEGEND

Dredger Tailings

Rocky Areas

Old River Channel

Underwater Shelf

Roads

SCALE

0   ½   1   2   3   4

N

CARRVILLE

Trinity R.

Copper Cr.

Coffee Cr.

East Fork Trinity River

Cedar Cr.

Squirrel Gul.

Nelson Cr.

To French Gul.

Hay Gul.

Jackass Springs Camp

Wyntoon Camp

Trinity Center Camp

TRINITY CENTER

Preacher Meadow Camp

Hatchet Cr.

N. Fk. Swift Cr.

Swift Cr.

③

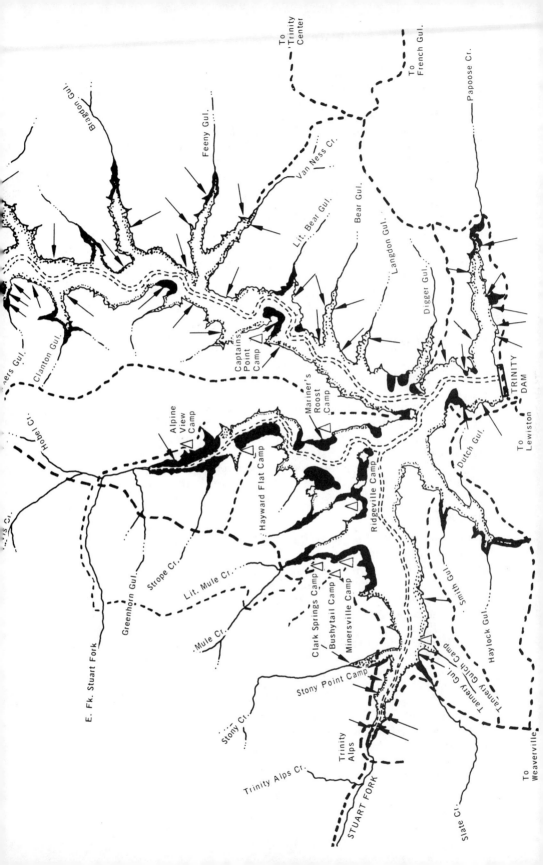

In the past several years of fishing Trinity Lake, I have kept notes on the different areas of the lake. Features that are not readily noted by the first-time or visiting angler will point up why fishing is good in one area and not so good in other areas. These notes are relatively complete, but they do not imply that you will not take at least some bass, providing you use the proper techniques, in all areas of the lake. Rather, it means that the ratio of success for a day of fishing will be better in areas that have the proper substructure on the bottom and the type of cover preferred by bass and panfish.

Forest Service Camps

In general, the forest service camps all around the lake have been built in areas that are the flattest available. This also usually means that there is an underwater shelf in the areas directly in front of these campsites extending for a distance out into the lake and providing good habitat for the bass.

Papoose Creek

The Papoose Creek area near the dam on the east side of the main lake is a good smallmouth bass area. The reason for this is because there are relatively more rocky areas. These rocky areas are sometimes small, so the angler looking for smallmouths should fish along a length of the shoreline where rocky areas are noted on the map. Then he will be certain that he is hitting the actual rocky points and slides at the high-water levels.

Also worthy of note here are the fingers of land that jut out into the lake on the point of land at the south end of Digger Gulch just north of Papoose Inlet. The fact that there is a considerable rocky section nearby means that this is a better smallmouth spot.

There is an access road for shore fishermen at thè head of Papoose Inlet.

Digger Gulch

Digger Gulch has a single rocky outcropping as noted. The series of points along the north shore in the lake outside the gulch are good bass areas and should be fished carefully at any stage of the season. These outcroppings between Bear Gulch and Digger Gulch are among the best in this section of the lake.

Bear Gulch

Bear Gulch is good because of the number of rocky areas. Of particular note here is the rocky area just inside the south point of the gulch. Better smallmouth hold in this area than in most in this part of the lake. In general, the south side of the gulch is best for bass fishing.

A single rough campsite is located halfway up the gulch on the south shore.

Van Ness Creek

The best part of Van Ness is the far upper end. The creek is spring fed and an inflow of cool water is available year around. This, combined with the fact that good, rocky habitat is available, makes this a key spot. There is an access road where cartop boats can be launched at the head of the gulch.

Feeny Gulch

The last half-mile of the gulch at

Feeny Gulch is the best fishing area here. The north shore is the best spot and the shallow point of land on the north edge of the point should be fished carefully. Bass lie along the flank of this underwater ridge.

Bragdon Gulch

Fish the south side of Bragdon Gulch and the far upper end of the gulch itself. At the upper end there is a large shallow area where bass find ideal spawning conditions during early summer. There is a single rough campsite on the south side halfway up the gulch. Fishing is good right outside this camp area.

Hay Gulch

Hay Gulch is best fished in the upper end. There is a long shallow area here that features rocky areas and some drowned brush during the high-water levels. There are large meadows here that, when drowned in the spring, provide shallow sections that warm up quicker than most sections of the lake. This means that bass will move onto these flats earlier to spawn than in most sections. The reason that this area warms sooner is that it is so protected from the winds. There are rough camps here.

Fish the rocky slide indicated between Hay Gulch and Bragdon Gulch. This is a particularly productive area for largemouths as well as smallmouths. It is necessary to cast close to the rocky slide and allow the lure or bait to drop straight down the steep shoal bank.

Jackass Islands

At high water two islands are visible off the point of the East Fork Inlet.

There are actually three islands here, but one, inside the mouth of the inlet, is awash at the high-water level. This entire area should be fished carefully and the area between the two islands visible at high water should be fished with extra care. Bass will be found around this entire area at all stages of the season.

East Fork

Note the few rocky areas and outcroppings along the south side of the East Fork Inlet. Fish these areas carefully. The best section to fish at all stages is the large rocky area on the far upper north shore and the large shallow area at the mouth of the East Fork River during the early part of the season. This shallow section is particularly good during the spawning season because there are such extensive shallows here that many bass move in to spawn. The East Fork is also noted for the amount of food and silt that it pours into the lake in the spring.

There is a rough shore camp of considerable size on the south side where the road to French Gulch crosses the East Fork. Cartop boats can be launched when the water is up.

Squirrel Gulch

Squirrel Gulch is much the same as the far upper reaches of the East Fork arm of the lake in that there is a large area of gently sloping underwater structure that warms quickly to spawning temperatures in the spring. This section is particularly good spawning for largemouths because there are few of the gravel or rock areas that smallmouths prefer.

There is an island at lower

In the East Fork arm, the angler will find one of the few areas at Trinity Lake where he can wade and cast to the fish. This area produces trout in the early spring when they are here to feed, but it is best to try for bass in this section.

water levels almost directly in the middle of the channel that is awash in the high-water period. Fish this area with care at any stage of the season because bass are always somewhere down its flanks.

There is an island just inside the north point of East Fork Inlet. Fish around this island, between it and the point, and especially at the rock slide visible at any stage of the season just outside the point. Bass lie along this steep ledge all year around and trout also prefer this area over the deep channel of the old river bed. Baits, lures, and particularly leadhead jigs are effective here. Some of the largest bass in the lake will be found along the face of this rocky cliff. Many anglers anchor here and fish straight down the cliff

face. Also fish the outcroppings noted along the east shore of the main Trinity in this area.

North Shore Tailings

Probably more smallmouths are taken fishing around the dredger tailing at the north end of the lake in the main Trinity arm of the lake than anywhere else. The tailing offers nearly perfect smallmouth habitat. Fishing with leadhead jigs, plastic worms, and nearly any kind of lure or bait is effective here for smallmouths. In the area of the tailings and the dredger ponds, separated from the main body of the lake, nearly any type of fishing is effective year around. In the hot summer months, the Trinity River pours in cool water to keep this section at good water temperatures for extended periods of the season.

There are camps and a rough launch area in this section.

Trinity Center

There is a huge area of shallows that slopes down into the lake from the north of Wyntoon Harbor to Scotts Marina off the Trinity Center shoreline. This slope is dotted with rocks and stumps and is a primary area for the bass fisherman. You can move along this shoreline for hours and fish endless good spots with the proper habitat for both species as well as for panfish. The fishing is good year around. Note also the dredger tailings and rocky areas in this shoreline area north of Wyntoon Harbor and in the first inlet north of Brush Creek.

Twin Gulch

South of Scotts Marina is Twin Gulch. The best spot here is the north point of the Twin Gulch inlet. There is developing rock along a relatively shallow slope. The south point of the inlet is notable because of the large number of stumps.

Packer Gulch

At Packer Gulch fish the upper end of the gulch where brush and a shallow slope provide good largemouth habitat. Fish the rocky south side for smallmouths. This is one of the better inlets in this section of the lake.

Billys Gulch

In Billys Gulch fish the side inlets and coves where the winter runoff has piled rubble.

Moore Gulch

Moore Gulch is best fished along the rocky north point and the underwater substructure around this long point. This is one of the best areas for bass in this arm of the lake.

Captains Point

At Captains Point there is a long finger of land that runs out into the lake right where the campground sign is located. The entire point is rocky, clear around the point to the next inlet. This is all developing rock and not large boulders, but smallmouths hold in this area.

Bowerman Point

Bowerman Point is an area of developing rock that is getting more extensive every season as the water of the open lake pounds it almost constantly. The slope of the underwater structure is also getting less pronounced and as time wears away this area, it will become a premium spot.

East Fork of the Stuart Fork

The main attraction for the black bass fisherman in the East Fork of the Stuart Fork area is the series of islands and underwater shelves around them between Ridgeville Camp Point and Mariners Roost Camp. These islands do not appear even on the official forest service map of this region, but they are very important to the bass fisherman because they supply so much ideal habitat for both largemouth and smallmouth bass.

I couldn't find any names for these islands so I've named them Pat's Islands for my wife, Pat Free-

A good trout like this one, taken on light tackle in a smaller stream like the Stuarts Fork, can be the challenge of a lifetime for the serious trout fisherman. The streams that empty into Trinity Lake are a fly fisherman's dream. In summer they run gin clear and you have to use very tender tackle.

man, because she has taken so many limits of bass during the peak of the spring fishing activity. The area right out in front of Mariners Roost Camp is also productive because of the ridge of developing rock that juts out here.

This area is easily reached by anglers camped at the numerous forest service camps in this section of the lake, so it gets more fishing pressure than most sections of Trinity Lake.

East Fork of Stuart

In the section of the lake near where the East Fork of the Stuart Fork flows into the lake, there is a large area of relatively shallow water due to siltation pouring into the lake during the high-water periods. This is an ideal spot for largemouths, especially during the spawning seasons. These silted outcroppings provide a perfect habitat for largemouth spawning. The East Fork also pours in a continual supply of both food and cool water for an extended period of time, enticing bass and other game fish to gather in large numbers here.

Rocky Point

The Rocky Point section of the Stuart Fork arm is, as its name implies, a very rocky area. Smallmouth bass fishing is excellent here because of this. The rocky areas extend almost to the point where the Stuart Fork enters the lake.

Stuart Fork

The section where the Stuart Fork enters the lake always produces bass and other game fish. This section, depending on the water level, has the fortunate combination of cool inflowing water laden with food and some rugged rocky sections.

The best sections of this arm to fish are those marked with underwater outcroppings and the scattered rocky sections noted on the map. In general, the north shore has produced the best bass fishing for me, particularly in the rocky areas.

From this area to the dam there are only a few outstanding sections.

The steepness of the shoreline along the south edge of the Stuart Fork arm makes the band of holding water so small in most cases that it is one of the more difficult to fish. However, the face of the dam is an excellent spot to fish and many fine limits are taken each year from this area.

The Upper Trinity

The upper Trinity River above Trinity Lake and the tributary streams to the upper river offer some very fine stream fishing for trout. The Trinity River in its upper sections drains a large area and the water here is extremely clear during the warm-water months. The upper

Good strings of trout can be taken from the river and streams above Trinity Lake. The best time to score on larger fish is during the spring months when the snow melt raises the water levels in these streams to the point where trout will move into them to feed and to spawn.

river also has runs of fish during the spring and fall that come out of the depths of the lake.

The huge 1964 flood that hit the entire north coast and the Trinity River in particular with a deluge greater than any other for the last 1,000 years did a great deal of damage to the streambed of the upper Trinity River and the feeder streams in this area. For the five years following this flood, the streams above Trinity Lake were virtually straight chutes of water running over rocks that had been completely denuded of all streamside brush and other trout cover. However, these streams have made a comeback from this disastrous flood and they again provide good trout fishing.

It takes time for soil to build up along the rocky shorelines of the river, but tufts of grass and streamside brush have taken hold in the streams above the lake. In the rocky areas where masses of rock have formed deeper water, the angler will find the best holding water for trout. In the areas where only rubble and smaller rocks are found, only smaller trout will be found during periods other than the spawning season of spring and late fall.

Little Trinity River

The Trinity River above Trinity Lake runs through the same type of flood plain as does the lower nine miles of Coffee Creek. The river provides good trout fishing up as far as its junction with Little Trinity River during the summer and fall months. Above this area the river is relatively small and the only time that fishing here is worth the effort is during the spring runoff months when the stream has a good head of water.

Little Trinity River carries a good head of water all year and few anglers bother to fish it. The river usually gives up trout that run from six to fourteen inches, but it is a scenic stream for the angler who likes to fish in intimate waters.

Eagle Creek

The best trout fishing in the upper Trinity River is from Eagle Creek to the spot where the river enters the lake. The section below the point where Coffee Creek enters the Trinity River has more water and more trout in it than the rest of the stream. Here, until the hot months of August and September, you can nearly always find good numbers of fair sized trout that have come up out of the lake. The river can be waded nearly anywhere and there are endless small pockets where trout can find fast food and safety. In the canyon section from the North Fork upstream, there are many deep holes that provide excellent trout holding water. In general, the larger stream trout will hold in these deeper pockets. Coffee Creek is too small in this area for effective lure fishing and bait or flies are the best method of fishing the stream.

The forks of Coffee Creek are also excellent trout fishing areas. Each stream can be fished from trails that run along the banks. The forks of the creek are basically the same type of stream as the main branch of Coffee Creek below the point where it joins the North Fork. This upper section of the creek and its tributaries all feature good trout holding pools that have been cut from the solid rock of the canyons through which they flow.

Coffee Creek Road

Coffee Creek Road is unique. The road not only offers anglers access

In selecting dry flies for fishing the streams above Trinity Lake, lay them out on the counter. A good dry fly has stiff hackles and the tail is of a length that doesn't allow the hook to touch at any spot. These streams are very rough flowing and good flies are essential.

to the entire length of the main branch of the creek but is one of the few roads that actually enters a wilderness area. The road runs through the Salmon–Trinity Alps Primitive Area set up by the U.S. Government and is one of the few exceptions to the primitive area rule that no motor driven vehicles may be used.

Coffee Creek

A mile or two above Trinity Lake, the upper Trinity River is joined by Coffee Creek. Coffee Creek provides a flow of water that is at least equal to that of the upper river itself. This creek has made a better recovery from the 1964 flood than the upper Trinity and supplies some of the best all-season trout fishing in this area.

The section of Coffee Creek nearest to the confluence with the Trinity River has several resorts on its bank and some of the stream is posted so that only guests of these resorts can fish. However, the bulk of Coffee Creek is open to public angling.

A good, all-weather road follows Coffee Creek, but in most cases access is difficult for the first dozen miles. The creek runs through a steep canyon here and the best access points are down the canyon wall at spots where secondary streams feed into Coffee Creek. At these spots the secondary streams have cut pathways along their course where you can gain access to

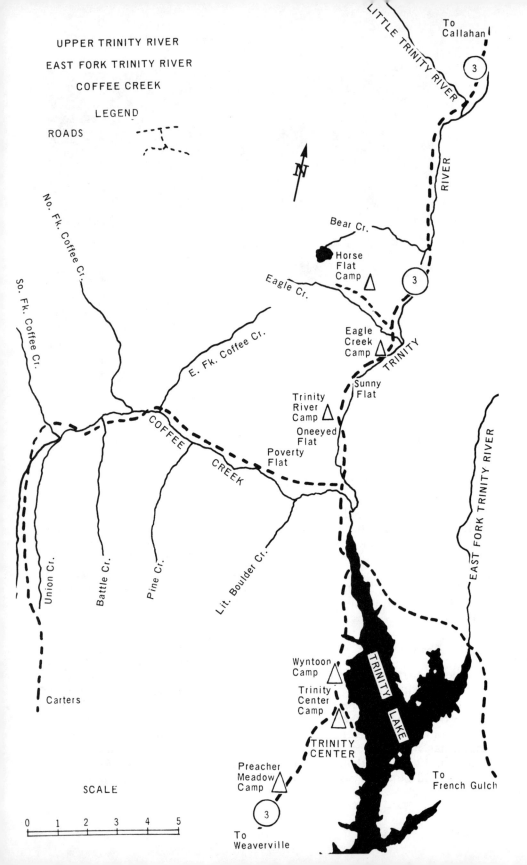

the creek by scaling down the banks of these secondary streams.

Approximately nine miles up Coffee Creek from the Trinity River, the nature of Coffee Creek changes a great deal. In the lower nine miles, the creek runs through a rubble streambed area. In this area the water cascades over relatively small rocks and boulders and fly fishing or bait fishing is about the only way you can fish the stream. There are a few spots where deeper holes have formed, but the bulk of the lower stream is comparatively shallow and the trout will be found primarily in the smaller pockets of water where the stream has routed out fairly shallow holes. Above the North Fork of Coffee Creek, the river runs through a hard rock canyon.

At the end of the road along Coffee Creek is Carters Resort. The resort nestles in an alpine valley studded with massive trees and brooding cliffs of granite. This area is so magnificently beautiful that I suggest anglers make a trip to this spot. The view from the resort of Caribou Mountain and Sawtooth Ridge is alone worth the trip. Also, the headwaters of the Salmon River originate in a series of lakes located about a mile above the resort. These lakes can be fished for beautiful little brook trout.

Josephine Lake

Josephine Lake is reached by making a stiff climb up the granite slope above Carters Resort. A fee is charged for ·fishing here, but it is worth it if the fisherman wants to try for the brookies.

Salmon River

The upper Salmon River on the resort property carries a good year-round head of water. The fishing for native rainbow trout is excellent here in the valley and along the cascading slope below Josephine Lake. A few of the brook trout come down into the stream in the spring, but they soon move downstream to get away from the fast-moving white water.

Wilderness Area

Fishing is excellent in all of the streams and lakes in the Salmon–Trinity Alps Wilderness Area. No travel is permitted by motor driven vehicles except in the Coffee Creek Road area. An angler must either hike into this area or be taken in on pack horses. There are many pack stations here.

Virtually all of the lakes are stocked with brook trout and it is no chore to take easy limits of these bright little fish. In general, the streams hold rainbow trout because brookies will not stay in the fast-moving white water that rainbows prefer. In most cases the lakes are actually overstocked with these brook trout. The average brookies will go to around six to nine inches in length.

East Fork

The East Fork of the Trinity River is unique because of the extremely thick population of caddis fly larva found here. The East Fork isn't a very large stream, but the heavy numbers of caddis cause excellent growth of the trout that either stay in the lower mile or two of the stream or come up out of the lake in order to feed on caddis flies. The East Fork is an extremely clear stream in the lower sections and it

This is the upper Trinity River just above where it joins Coffee Creek in the Oneeyed Flat area. During the summer, the angler can quarter the stream almost anywhere, but in the spring the river is a large stream. Fish in the side currents where trout stay to keep out of the main current.

is necessary to use very fine tackle to the fish. A leader that tests more than two pounds will rarely take trout from this stream.

Access to the East Fork is gained from the bridge on French Gulch Road where it crosses the East Fork. There is a rough campsite located on the south bank of the stream just downstream from this bridge. Some of the best pools and riffles in the East Fork are located here. The road that heads upstream for a short distance has one access point across Southern Pacific property, but the rest of the shore is held by ranchers and posted. Most of this section of the stream is so small that

it is only worth fishing in the very early season for spawners that have come up out of the lake.

Trinity River Phone Numbers

In fishing for steelheads and salmon, it is important for the angler to make contacts on the stream in order to be able to tell if there are any fish running in the river at the time a trip is planned. This is even true when it comes to fishing lakes like Trinity and Lewiston Lakes. However, lake fishing information is not nearly as important as river fishing information because the fish in the lakes are not migratory, except when they are spawning in tributaries.

An angler who lives some distance from the Trinity River will want to phone ahead before making a long and costly trip to the river. A simple phone call is insurance for the fisherman.

In this section of the guide, I have listed phone numbers of businessmen who service anglers and tourists visiting the Trinity River streams and lakes. These people make their living this way and they know that happy anglers return again and again.

Deep Sleep Motel, Hoopa,
  916-625-4268
The Oaks Cafe, Hoopa,
  916-625-4296
Sports N Spirits, Willow Creek,
  916-629-2462

Elkhorn Motel, St. Helena,
  916-623-6318
Morris Hardware, Weaverville,
  916-623-2952
Weaverville Hotel, Weaverville,
  916-623-3121
Indian Creek Motel, Douglas
  City, 916-623-6294
Stott Enterprises, Douglas City,
  916-623-6155
Lewiston Hotel, Lewiston,
  916-778-3823
Lakeview Terrace, Lewiston,
  916-778-3803
Pine Cove Park, Lewiston,
  916-778-3838
Wyntoon Park, Trinity Center,
  916-266-3337
Scott's Marina, Trinity Center,
  916-266-3324

California Steelhead Rivers

The streams that are included in this section of the guide—coastal waters from Monterey Bay to the Oregon border—are what are known in California as the winter group. Most of these streams are comparatively small rivers during the summer and early fall months. But when the winter rains begin, they swell in size and provide some of the best steelheading to be found in California.

The streams of the north coast are particularly attractive for the steelheader. Even the smallest has a large tidal basin near the mouth.

They vary in length from the short tidal streams like the Garcia or the Gualala to lengthy rivers like the Eel and the Russian, which drain vast areas. The variety of fishing situations and conditions are wide in individual rivers and vast throughout the entire system of rivers.

Smith River

The Smith River, the first California stream south of the Oregon border with good steelhead runs, is noted not only for its number of winter-

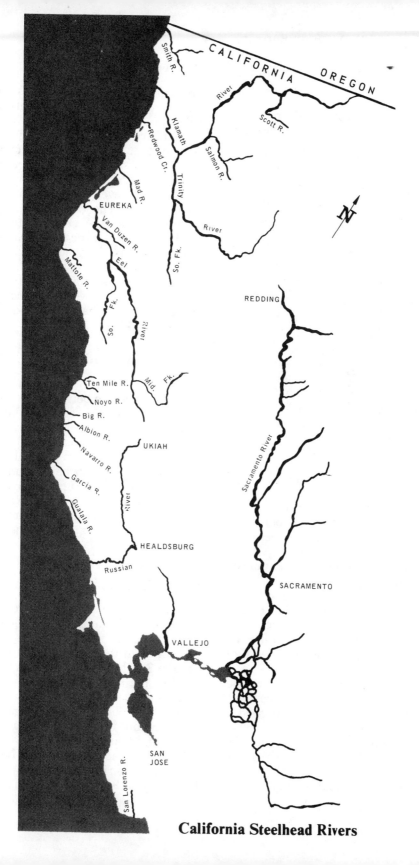

California Steelhead Rivers

and late fall-run steelheads but also for the size of the average fish taken here.

The Smith River is an unusually clear stream any time of the year. The river basin drains an extremely rocky area. The river has chewed down through what amounts to bedrock in most areas to form the river bed. This also means the Smith river is a quick clearing stream after all but the largest of winter storms. In most cases the river will be clear and fishable within a few days of a sizable storm, while the rest of the streams along the north coast are still roiled.

November is usually the beginning of the Smith River steelheading. Earlier in the year, from September on, the stream is noted for large salmon. Of particular interest is the fly fishing for these winter-run king salmon. Some of these, taken on fly rods, have weighed fifty pounds.

Lower Smith River

Below the Dr. Fine Memorial Bridge on Highway 101, the best steelhead fishing takes place in the series of riffles and holes from just below the bridge to Piling Hole. The holes here change from year to year and either fill in or dig out depending on the currents and flow of the river during storms. Even though holes and riffles change location due to the silting and dredging action of the river, they usually either reform in another nearby spot or come back the following year.

You can launch a skiff just below the Dr. Fine Bridge on the north bank. Cautious wading is needed in all the fishing areas of the lower river. Smith River fishermen normally do their fishing from a skiff. A dike system now cuts off most of the sloughs in the tidal section.

Between the Bridges

Probably more large steelheads are taken from the series of beautiful riffles and pools between the Highway 101 Bridge and the Highway 199 Bridge than in any other comparable length of steelhead water in California. This stretch of river, approximately seven miles long, is all good fishing. The deep holes are formed where the river collides with huge rocks or the rocky banks. The river has dredged out deep holes that provide excellent holding water for both steelheads and salmon. The riffles between these holes and along gravel bars are good fly fishing areas.

North Bank Road

Highway 197 runs along the north bank of the Smith between the two bridges. There are access points where the road runs beside the river. The key access points are Simpson Camp and the county park along this road. The north bank road is used for access to the upper portion of this stretch of the Smith River and the road along the south bank is used for access near the Highway 101 Bridge.

South Bank Road

The road along the south bank turns off Highway 101 at the south end of the bridge. A short distance upstream from the bridge road turnoff, the South Bank Road leads to a road system along the gravel bars. These gravel bar roads change after every flood or high-water stage in the river, but they lead to the good fishing holes and riffles.

There is access to a deep hole and a series of riffles and runs at the Highway 199 Bridge. Access is

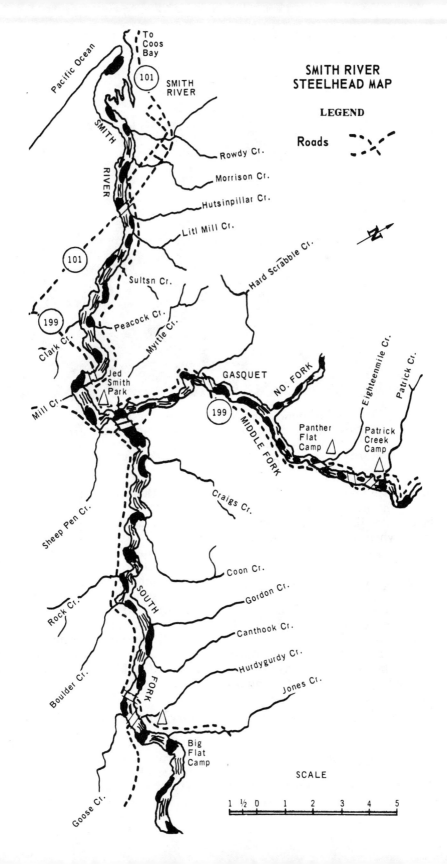

In the upstream section of coastal rivers, larger fish like this one are a challenge. Steelies usually change their feeding habits in the upstream part of the river and darker flies are in order. Long casts are not usually needed to fish this section of stream.

down the steep bank at the north end of the bridge. Hiouchi Hole just below the bridge is particularly good when steelheads are laying over in this area.

Highway 197 to South Fork

The best access to the short stretch of stream between the Highway 199 Bridge and the South Fork is through the state park on the north side of the river. This area of stream is about the same as that found below, between the two bridges, with Mill Creek Hole the primary holding area.

Mill Creek Road

The South Fork Road heads across both forks of the river just above Myrtle Creek. This road forks on the south bank of the South Fork. The Mill Creek Road heads back downstream for a few miles until it connects with Mill Creek and heads away from the river. There is an excellent series of deep, broken riffles that are good fly and bait water one mile from the point where the Mill Creek Road heads along the river. Access is directly to the river from this road. This road provides access to Stout Grove.

Forks of Smith

At the forks of the Smith River, there are some very deep holes that have steelheads in them for nearly the entire season. These are holding pools and are best fished with lures or baits. Access to other pools in this area is blocked completely by steep, sheer banks. It may be necessary to scale high bluffs in order to fish along the river. There are falls a half-mile up the South Fork. On the main river there are steep trails down the bluff to the lower holes. There is access to both the South Fork and the Middle Fork at the bridges on the South Fork Road.

South Fork Access

The South Fork Road runs along the river, but in many places the road climbs up along the ridge and access is either impossible or extremely steep. However, there are several places along this fifteen-mile stretch of road to Jones Creek, the upper limit of winter fishing, where access is possible.

The lower few miles of the South Fork run through bedrock. There are very deep holes and short whitewater riffles here. This is the best section of the Smith South Fork for the bait or lure fisherman. In the upper reaches of the South Fork, many landslides have filled in the streambed. This area is better for the fly fisherman.

Gasquet

Between the South Fork and Hardscrabble Creek, the Middle Fork of the Smith is serviced by Highway 199. In places it is necessary to scale a steep trail, but access to nearly all of this water is possible. The water below Hardscrabble Creek is mainly bedrock holes, short white water, and deep riffles. Fly fishing can be good here, but lures and baits work better in the deep holes.

From Hardscrabble Creek to Gasquet the river changes in char-

acter. This area is good for fly fishing. The pools are not as deep here. Fish toward the banks where rocks have formed deeper pockets.

North Fork

The North Fork is open for a mile or so from its junction with the Smith River. To gain access to the North Fork, cross the Middle Fork at Middle Fork Road. You can head down the Middle Fork to get to the North Fork. A trail at the top of the ridge off Middle Fork Road leads down to the junction of the North and Middle Forks of the Smith. The trail takes off from the south side of the road just past a sign reading Berry Lane. You have the right trail if you pass two gravesites.

Upper Middle Fork

Winter fishing is allowed as far up the Middle Fork as Patrick Creek. There are campgrounds and bridges that allow direct access. Much of the river can be reached directly from Highway 199. This stretch of the Smith River is good for fly fishing and some of the deeper holes are good bait water. In general, this section is not holding water except for a few spots such as in the deep holes at the mouth of creeks like Eighteen Mile Creek and Kelly Creek. There are campgrounds along the road and a few rough sites where the old highway used to run. These can be seen from the road. There are several bridges on the Middle Fork, each of which provides access to the river.

Redwood Creek

Redwood Creek is included in this steelhead fishing guide because it can be a very good fishing area, providing the angler is able to be on the spot when the steelheads are in the creek. Redwood Creek is a now-and-then type of stream. The creek drains a huge area; rains that fall here can be torrential. This means the creek floods rapidly after a storm of any real size. There has been so much lumbering activity in this drainage that it takes a considerable amount of time for the creek to clear after a sizable storm.

The important section of Redwood Creek for the visiting angler is the few miles of stream below Prairie Creek. This creek carries a good head of water year around and many of the steelheads that enter Redwood Creek break off from the main watershed and enter Prairie Creek. Steelies that enter the drainage will gang up in the tidal area and the lower few miles of stream to wait for a storm. This puts them under the gun for the angler.

Tidal Lagoon

The main access point to the tidal lagoon at the mouth of Redwood Creek is through the county park a few miles south of the city of Orick. You can park in the parking lot at the park or drive down the beach almost to the water's edge. There are rough campsites on the sandbar here.

The tidal lagoon of Redwood Creek is typical of tidal lagoons in all of the rivers along the coast. It

Even small streams like Redwood Creek can deal up large fish during the winter months. This brace of steelies was landed by fishing along the brushy shoreline where pockets have formed under the sweepers.

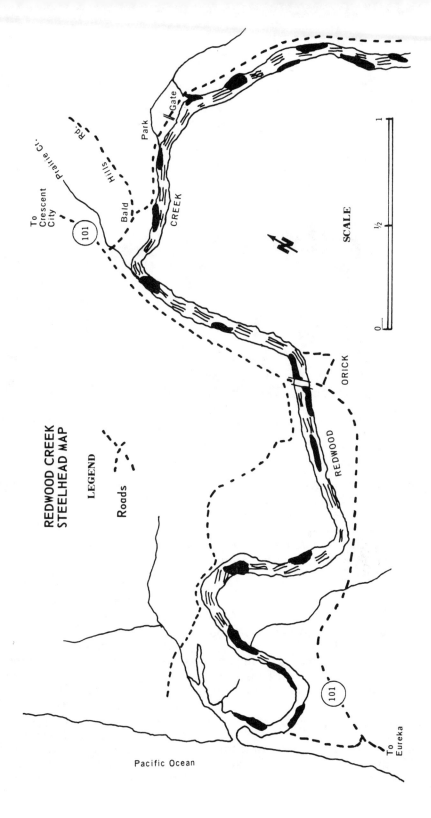

REDWOOD CREEK
STEELHEAD MAP

LEGEND

Roads

SCALE

0   ½   1

To Crescent City

To Crescent City   Prairie Cr. Rd.

Bald Hills Rd.

Park

Gate

CREEK

101

ORICK

REDWOOD

Pacific Ocean

101

To Eureka

The tidal section of coastal streams is often wide, even on smaller streams. It is necessary to move around a great deal in order to find the spots where steelies hold in these tidal lagoons.

features large masses of water when the tides are in and good run-outs as the tides enter and leave. The area is mostly sand dunes. There is a dike system in the upper stretches. Access is along the sand and rock bank.

Orick Dike Access

The dike system that protects the town of Orick offers easy access between the tidal lagoon and the upper river. The access is direct from the roads in this area.

Bald Hills Road

Bald Hills Road turns off east from Highway 101 just north of Orick and heads along the creek. Approxi-mately one half mile from the Highway 101 junction, the road begins to climb away from the creek bank, but an access road along the creek for another half mile services this area. The National Park Service has blocked this road, which formerly allowed anglers to drive to the upper limit of fishing. The angler must park and walk upstream if he wants to fish this area.

It is debatable whether it is worth the visiting angler's time to try fishing above the mouth of Prairie Creek. It is essential that timing for fishing this area be exact because steelheads that enter the main stream from the tidal lagoon move quickly through the lower river to the canyon stretches upstream. A visiting angler does not stand much chance of hitting this area at precisely the right stage of the runoff. However, if an angler does hit this area at the right time, he can have good fishing.

Mad River

Like most coastal streams that have steelheads during the late fall and winter months, the Mad River is usually most productive for the visiting angler in the tidal sections. There is good access to the lower river for the angler who wants to fish from a small boat.

Lower River Access

By taking the Janes Road exit from Highway 101 to the west, the angler will see signs directing him to Mad River Beach. Follow these signs. There are a few access points along this road, but fishing in these areas is not very good.

There is a rough road system down the bars near the angling access area that can be used by shore fisherman to fish the lower stretches of the Mad. Most of this road system is over raw sand and care should be used in taking passenger vehicles very far.

There are parking spaces and another rough road system at the swimming beach, which can be used for anglers for fishing near the mouth. Care should be used when driving this road system, also.

Upstream Access

At the Highway 101 Bridge there is an access road, the North Bank Road, that skirts the river. Some of the best pool and riffle water can be reached from this road. Access to the river is direct from the North Bank Road until its junction with Highway 299. Just downstream from the Highway 299 Bridge across the Mad there is a road that takes off from the North Bank Road and heads under the Highway 299 Bridge to an area that features many big rocks and deep holding pools. This area, and the few miles of stream reached from this access point either by using the road system along the bars or by walking, is one of the finest on the Mad River.

West End Road

West End Road follows the south bank of the Mad River between the junction with Highway 299 and the town of Blue Lake. There are several access points on West End Road, the best of which are at the Humboldt County Pumping Stations. These are areas with deep holes near the pumps that hold steelheads any time the fish are in this area.

Highway 299 Access

There are access points at all of the off-ramps from Highway 299 along its length between the bridge and Blue Lake on the north shore. Much of the stream can be reached from these points.

Hatchery Road

Hatchery Road out of Blue Lake crosses the river. There are extensive road systems along the bar both upstream and down. The river in this area is primarily a wandering, fairly shallow stream with the exception of a few holes, such as the deep hole directly under the bridge on Hatchery Road. Access upstream is blocked by a private lumber company road east of Blue Lake.

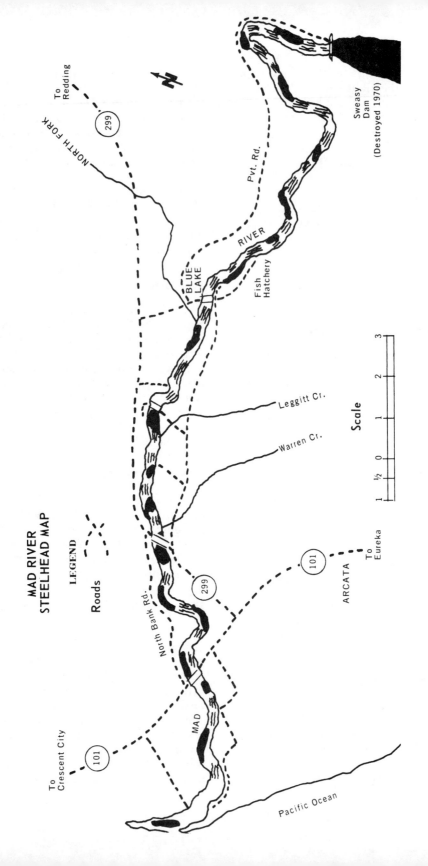

A typical brace of winter-run steelies. Note here the meat rod used for ultimate distance casting in the tidal sections of coastal streams. Properly rigged, these big rods and level wind reels will cover more water than any other type of gear.

Salmon River

The Salmon River is one of those special steelhead streams that has fish in it virtually the entire year. It drains much of the northern half of the Salmon–Trinity Alps Wilderness Area. This means the waters of the South Fork remain very cool and clear the year around. This is the reason the South Fork has runs of steelies even during the very hot months of July and August.

In two sections of the river the stream cuts through a very deep gorge and for several miles access is almost impossible, except in a few spots. The river, especially the South Fork, changes character several times. In some areas it is a relatively placid stream that flows through a wide, gravel flood plain. In these spots the best bet is to fish against the large rocks that dot the shoreline and poke up in midstream. The action of the flowing water has routed out deep pockets at the base of these rocks and this is where the steelheads hole up.

In the canyon sections of the stream, virtually the entire river is one long series of very deep holes. The lure and bait fisherman can have a field day if he locates a run of steelies in this deep pool water. The fly fisherman is put on his mettle in this area and the premium is on deep sinking flies and deep sinking fly lines.

Ishi Pishi Bridge

The first access point to the Salmon

River is off the Ishi Pishi Bridge Road. This road takes off north from Somes Bar from the Klamath River Highway at a small store and gas station about a mile from the Highway 96 bridge across the Salmon River. There is a huge hole where the river enters the Klamath and steelheads hold in this area. This access also leads to the Highway 96 bridge.

Highway 96 Bridge

At the Highway 96 bridge there is access to the Salmon River. This area features fairly deep holes with long glides and relatively shallow pools. Fish near the base of the rocks and where the river twists to touch rocky shorelines.

Oak Bottom Camp

Oak Bottom is a huge forest service campsite. There is excellent access to the same type of water that is found in the lower section of the stream. Oak Bottom Camp is 1.3 miles along the east bank road from the Highway 96 bridge.

Three Dollar Bar

There is an access point at Three Dollar Bar, 1.1 miles above Oak Bottom Camp. The first really deep pool on the Salmon River is located here. This is mostly a bait pool, but this is the first spot where the steelies usually hole up and rest after leaving the pool at the mouth. This is one of the best spots on the lower river when the water is clear.

First Bridge

The first bridge across the lower Salmon River is located 1.2 miles above Three Dollar Bar and is an access point. About a quarter of a mile above this bridge is the Steinacher Creek Bridge. The first of the deep pools of the first gorge of the Salmon River begins here. The Steinacher and First Bridge both offer access to both sides of the river. The actual gorge starts three-tenths mile above the bridge.

Duncan Creek

At Duncan Creek there is good access 2.7 miles above the Steinacher Bridge. Here you will find typical canyon water with deep pools and deep runs of water connecting them. Any type of fishing equipment will work in these areas.

Butler Creek

Butler Creek is located one mile above Duncan Creek and offers access to the same type of water as is found at Duncan Creek.

Grant Creek

Grant Creek is special. It offers access to two of the higher falls on the lower river. There are some extremely deep holes here. Steelheads hole up in this area, especially during the summer months and during any stage of the runs when there is clear water.

Landslide

In 1964 a huge landslide dropped into the Salmon River during the big flood. It is located 1.8 miles above Grant Creek. This became a problem for the Department of Fish and Game because almost every winter the river cuts a channel that made a falls too high for fish to

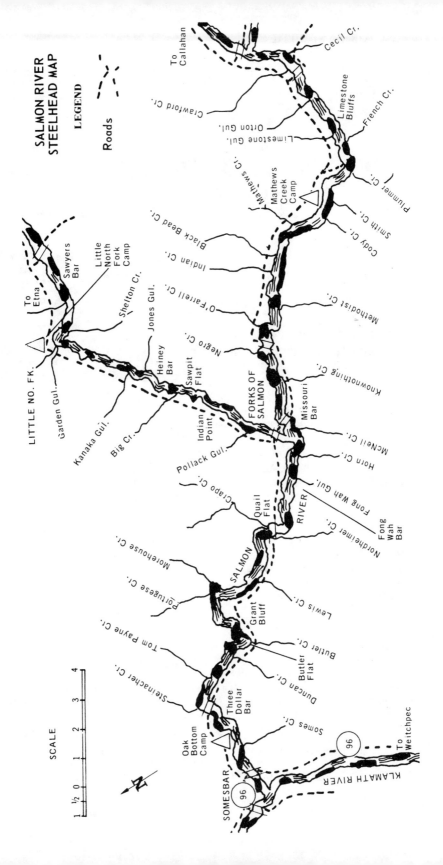

SALMON RIVER STEELHEAD MAP

LEGEND

Roads

SCALE

1 ½ 0   1   2   3   4

To Callahan

Cecil Cr.

Crawford Cr.

Limestone Gul.

Orton Gul.

Limestone Bluffs

French Cr.

Plummer Cr.

Smith Cr.

Cody Cr.

Mathews Cr.

Mathews Creek Camp

Black Bead Cr.

Indian Cr.

Methodist Cr.

O'Farrell Cr.

Negro Cr.

Knownothing Cr.

To Etna

Sawyers Bar

Little North Fork Camp

Shelton Cr.

Jones Gul.

Heiney Bar

Sawpit Flat

LITTLE NO. FK.

Garden Gul.

Kanaka Gul.

Big Cr.

Indian Point

Pollack Gul.

Crapo Cr.

FORKS OF SALMON

Missouri Bar

McNeil Cr.

Horn Cr.

Fong Wah Gul.

Fong Wah Bar

Quail Flat

RIVER

Nordheimer Cr.

SALMON

Morehouse Cr.

Portugese Cr.

Grant Bluff

Lewis Cr.

Tom Payne Cr.

Butler Cr.

Butler Flat

Duncan Cr.

Steinacher Cr.

Three Dollar Bar

Somes Cr.

Oak Bottom Camp

SOMESBAR

96

96

To Weitchpec

KLAMATH RIVER

The author's rig, used for home base while getting the detailed information for these guides. A trail bike goes on the front of the truck for checking out every road that leads to the water.

jump. This problem is now solved. There is a small falls here. Access is down the flanks of the slide.

Second Bridge

The Second Bridge offers access 1.1 miles above the landslide. The river changes character here to pool and glide water such as that found near the mouth.

Access Point

There is an access point 1.4 miles above Second Bridge down the east bank. The river is the same here as at Second Bridge.

Forks of Salmon — North Fork

There are two bridges at Forks of Salmon that offer access to the lower stretches of the North Fork and the South Fork. These bridges are nine-tenths of a mile above the last access point. There is a good pool at the mouth of the North Fork that holds steelies that will go up the North Fork. The South Fork water is relatively cool until late fall and the steelheads that go up the North Fork are reluctant to enter this stream until the water warms on the South Fork.

Dredger Tailing

There is access over a dredger tailing 1.6 miles above the Forks of Salmon Bridge. In this area, to Knownothing Creek access nine-tenths of a mile further upstream, the stream meanders and there are typical canyon holes with deep riffles between.

Third Bridge

At Third Bridge the stream meanders over a wide flood plain and it is not holding water. Third Bridge is one-half mile above the dredger tailing. There is a rough camp one mile above the dredger tailing access.

Methodist Creek

Access at Methodist Creek is 1.4 miles above Third Bridge. This is not holding water, but fishing can be good if steelies are moving through the area.

Falls

There is a steep access point to the falls one-half mile above Methodist Creek Steelies rest in the pools above and below the falls.

Indian Creek

There is an access point at Indian Creek 2.4 miles above Methodist Creek.

Black Bear Creek

At Black Bear Creek there is access at the mouth of the creek and for the next one-half mile upstream to some good pool water. It is eight-tenths of a mile from Indian Creek.

Mathews Creek

At Mathews Creek the gorge of the South Fork begins. It is 1.5 miles from Black Bear Creek.

South Fork Gorge

Some of the finest water on the entire Salmon River will be found in the South Fork Gorge. There are only three access points to the gorge, which is 5.2 miles long. One is located 2.2 miles above Mathews Creek. Park on the road and walk down past a chained off road block. Another is at Butcher Gulch three miles above Mathews Creek down an access road and another at Plummer Creek where you park on the highway and walk down. The gorge is made up mostly of deep pools and fast runs between the pools. Steelheads hold in all sections.

Cecilville

The upper bridge at Cecilville is the upstream limit of fishing during the winter season. There are few minor holes here. Cecilville Bridge is 36.6 miles above the Highway 96 Bridge.

North Fork of Salmon

The North Fork is only good during the winter months. I prefer to fish the lower four miles of the stream. There is little holding water in the North Fork between its mouth and the upstream limit of legal fishing at Sawyers Bar. The only time it is good is when migrations are on. Access is limited by the fact that the road climbs away from the river repeatedly, but when the road is at riverside access points are obvious.

Scott River

The Scott River is a special salmon spawning area during the fall months, but it is open to steelhead fishing from the middle of November through the last day in February. A few steelheads enter the Scott in the late summer and early fall, but few anglers do much fishing for these early-run fish. At this time of year, the waters of the Scott are extremely clear and usually very warm. The steelies are difficult to take.

However, fly and bait fishing is fairly good in the lower four miles above where the Scott enters the Klamath River. When the water is clear, it is necessary to fish with very light terminal tackle. Steelheads can be taken any time after the middle of July in the lower river by fishing very early and very late in the day. This small run of steelies is worth fishing for at this time of year only if the angler happens to be in the area. I've had my best luck using smaller than usual flies dressed on No. 6, No. 8, and No. 10 patterns. Larger flies are not nearly as effective. I also like my flies dressed very lightly at this time of year.

Lower Scott River

The lower few miles of the Scott River is made up of a series of deep pools interspersed with relatively shallow riffles. Steelies generally hold in the forward ends of these pools, which are easily spotted once you reach the river.

Take the old bridge a quarter of a mile above the junction with the Klamath River and cross over to the west bank. Access here is total for the next few miles until the bridge that spans the river again joins the west bank road about three miles above the old bridge. Access is also good in the last mile below this highway bridge on the Scott River Road on the east bank of the river. Several good riffles and holes can be fished from this side. There are plenty of parking spaces here.

Scott Bar

Access is good on the west side all the way to Scott Bar. The holes and riffles just below Scott Bar and just above the bridge that spans the river here are worth special attention. These are among the deepest holes in the entire lower river.

Townsend Gulch

The Scott River Road climbs away from the river and follows the ridge line for the next several miles. Access is extremely difficult. Most of this area is under private ownership and heavily posted. The banks here are extremely steep.

At Townsend Gulch the road again returns to the Scott and access is good along this section to Forest Service Road No. 46N64. This area is noted for very deep holes and portions of deep runs and riffles between holes. This is a holdover area. You will nearly always find some steelies in the deep pools. You can utilize flies, lures, or bait in this area with equal effectiveness.

Thompson Creek

The entire Scott River is accessible from Townsend Gulch to Thompson Creek, a distance of several miles. Most of this area is in forest service lands and access is total. All of this stretch of the Scott features very deep holes interspersed by quick, choppy riffles or deep glides of water. You will find every type of holding water here. This is some of the finest steelhead fishing water in the state when the steelies are running, generally during early November through Christmas.

Scott Valley

Above Thompson Creek the Scott River runs through Scott Valley. It

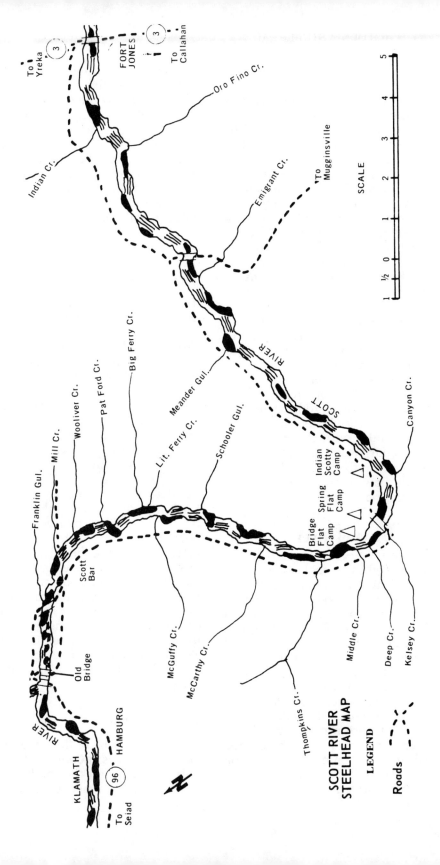

SCOTT RIVER
STEELHEAD MAP

LEGEND

Roads

is a typical meadow stream in this area. Access is good in the lower few miles of the river and there is some classic fly and bait water. Heavy fly fishing equipment isn't needed because the cast that will be made is relatively short.

In the lower portion of the river, about three miles above the canyon section, several seeps enter the river, which tend to cool the water and attract steelies. However, nowhere in the valley will you find typical holding water. The steelheads you do take will be transient fish moving through the valley toward the headwaters of the Scott.

Access is rare and through private property in the main Scott Valley up to the bridge at Fort Jones. The bridge at Fort Jones is the upper limit of fishing after the middle of November. This upstream area is hardly worth fishing during the summer months because so much of the water is taken out of the river for irrigation purposes. It almost amounts to a creek rather than a river. Steelheads spawn in the month of March and then leave the river.

Eel River

Many anglers wrongly believe fishing for steelheads in the Eel River has not been good since the 1964 flood. The flood did not ruin the Eel River; it merely changed it to such an extent that anglers who had fished it for years no longer knew where the fishing would be best.

Like any other steelhead stream, the Eel can reward the angler who works its waters when conditions are right. No steelhead river is innately good or bad. If the fish are not running, fishing will be poor. The Eel is no different from any other stream in this respect.

The main thing to consider when fishing the longer coastal streams such as the Eel is that you can be relatively certain there will be steelheads somewhere in the river after fall. The trick is to find the spots where the steelheads are holding. Access is the key to good steelhead fishing. In the case of the Eel River drainage, the complication is that there is so much water to be covered.

Lower Eel River

The Eel River was changed greatly by the 1964 flood. Where once there were a large number of areas that featured willows and other growth close to the water's edge, there are now few of these spots to aid the angler in locating holding water. The river flows through a sand and gravel area below the South Fork and a successful angler has to keep moving in order to locate runs of fish in this section.

There is even a modest run of early steelheads that enters the Eel River in early fall, about the first of September. This run normally doesn't have a lot of fish in it, but by carefully working the tidal section below Singley Bar the angler can usually earn some good strings of fish. The angler can fish from a boat in the lower stretches of the stream or from the road systems that lace the bars of the lower river. If an angler merely fishes a few spots, he lowers his chances of taking these early-run fish.

Cannibal Road

On the north bank of the Eel River, the first access is at Cannibal Road. This road ends on the sandbar at North Bay. It has an adequate launch

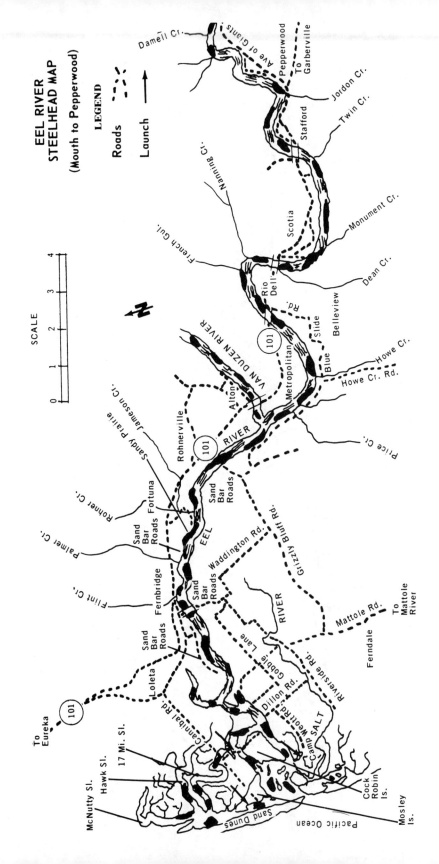

EEL RIVER
STEELHEAD MAP
(Mouth to Pepperwood)

LEGEND

Roads

Launch

SCALE

0 1 2 3 4

N

Damell Cr.

Ave of Giants

Pepperwood

To Garberville

Jordon Cr.

Twin Cr.

Stafford

Monument Cr.

Scotia

Manning Cr.

Dean Cr.

French Gul.

Rio Dell

Belleview

Slide

Blue

Howe Cr.

Howe Cr. Rd.

101

Metropolitan

Rd.

101

Price Cr.

Alton

VAN DUZEN RIVER

RIVER

Rohnerville

Jameson Cr.

Sandy Prairie

Rohner Cr.

Palmer Cr.

Fortuna

Sand Bar Roads

EEL

Sand Bar Roads

Waddington Rd.

Grizzly Bluff Rd.

RIVER

To Mattole River

Mattole Rd.

Ferndale

Riverside Rd.

Gobbie Lane

Dillon Rd.

Westrd.

Camp SALT

Flint Cr.

Fernbridge

Sand Bar Roads

Sand Bar Roads

Loleta

Cannibal Rd.

101

To Eureka

17 Mi. Sl.

Hawk Sl.

McNutty Sl.

Sand Dunes

Pacific Ocean

Cock Robin Is.

Mosley Is.

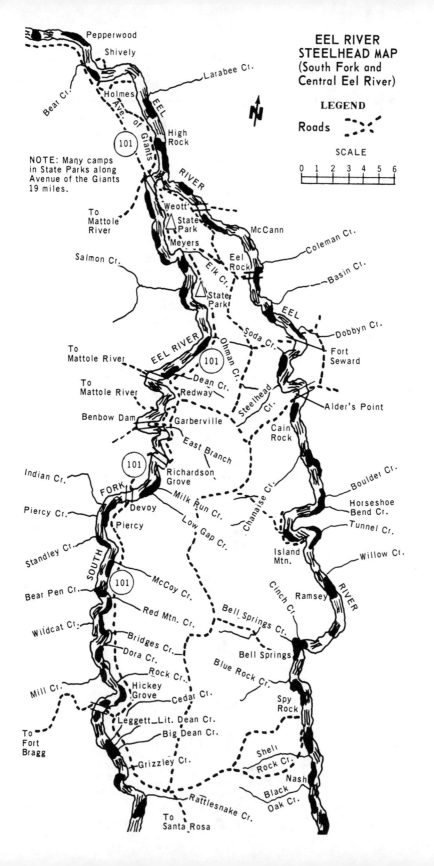

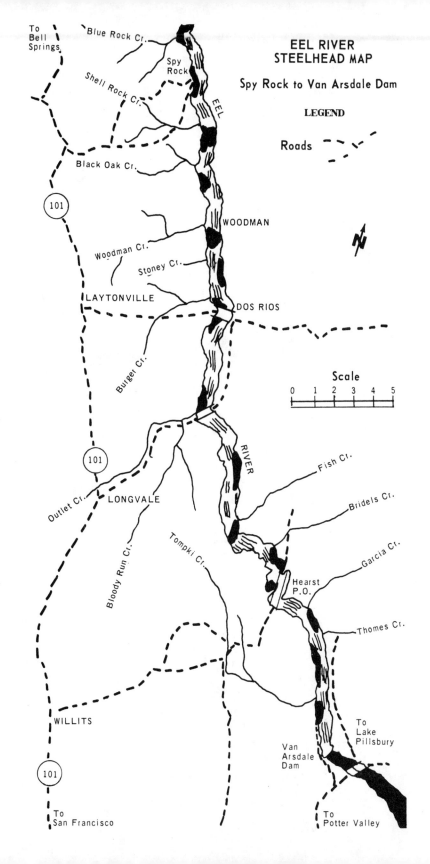

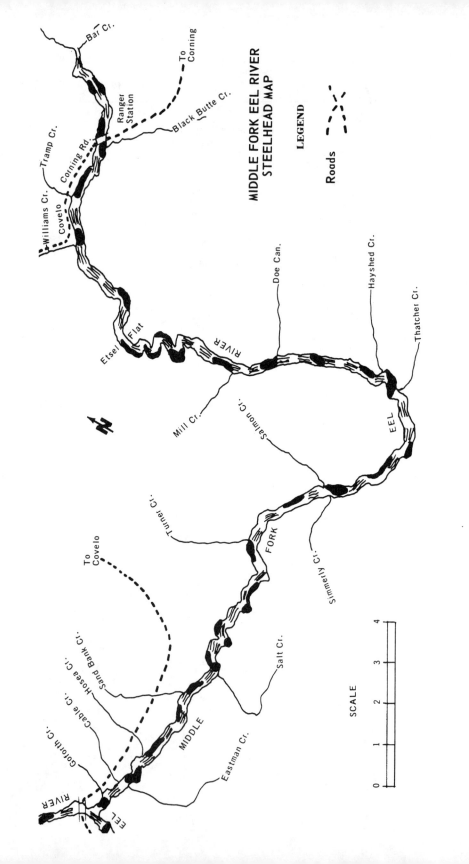

MIDDLE FORK EEL RIVER
STEELHEAD MAP

LEGEND

Roads

SCALE

0 1 2 3 4

area. There are some rough camps on the sandbar.

Cannibal Road leads out of the town of Loleta and a short distance down this road it joins Cock Robin Road. This road leads south to a narrow bridge to Cock Robin Island. It spans the slough. At the north end of this bridge, there is another rough launch site where small boats can be put into the water to fish in the slough and the main river. The end of this road is on the shore of the main Eel River. Access is by foot.

Singley Bar

There is an extensive road system at Singley Bar. A series of rough roads can be reached through the sand and gravel operation owned by Humboldt County. Singley Road takes off from the road to Loleta at the off-ramp from the freeway.

Camp Weott Road

On the south shore there are several access points. The first is Camp Weott Road. This road ends at the sandbar at the mouth of the river and has a rough launch site adequate for most boats.

In this same south bank area, Dillon Road and Fulmore Road offer access points. At Dillon Road you walk to the water across a long bar. At Fulmore Road there is an extensive rough road system. You can drive to the water across the bar. These are the only direct access points to the lower river from the south side below Fernbridge.

Grizzly Bluff Road

Grizzly Bluff Road leads to a rough road system on the bar above Fernbridge. Here the river is a typical wandering stream with a gravel bed and few obstructions. Upstream from this point, there are two access points on the road between Fernbridge and Rio Dell. They are at a riprap area on Weymouth Road and for a mile downstream from this point. There are some deep holes against the bluff upstream from this spot that are worth fishing. The last direct access point north of Rio Dell is at Howe Creek, where access is down the creek bed to the Eel.

Fernbridge Access

There are short access roads to the river bars on both sides of Fernbridge. The one on the southeast side takes off on the downstream side and is marked Waddington Road. The road on the other side leads to a rough road system on the bar on the highway side of the river. This access point is three-quarters of a mile upstream from the bridge.

Fortuna

Access is limited near Fortuna. There is an access area at the 12th Street off-ramp from Highway 101. You can walk past the sewage treatment plant for access down the bank or you can drive along the road that follows the west bank of Black Creek to limited access down the Fortuna Levee. At Drake Hill Road access is limited to the levee.

Van Duzen Access

The access point for fishing near the mouth of the Van Duzen and along its lower section is at the north end of the Highway 101 Bridge.

The area near the mouth of the Van Duzen is very important. Steelheads lie in the deeper pools in this area waiting for the Van Duzen to

The famous Fernbridge section of the Eel River is a gathering spot for steelheads and steelhead fishermen. The action of the current working against the bridge abutments has dredged out good holding pools. Anglers can fish these from the shelf of the abutment.

raise its water level so they can migrate into it. I have fished this spot a few times just as a rain starts and have had some great fishing. The pools change from year to year, but you can be sure there are steelies holding somewhere in this area any time during the late fall and winter.

Sheppard

There are some good pools and riffles with the first traces of rocks at Sheppard. Access is on the south end of the Sheppard Bar through a gravel operation.

Stafford and Avenue of the Giants

Where the highway crosses the Eel just above Stafford, the Avenue of the Giants intersects Highway 101. The Avenue is actually the old highway. It generally follows the course of the river and can be used to gain access to the length of the river in this section.

At the north or downstream end of the Avenue, the old highway dead ends into the river bank. There are access points to some good pool and riffle water off the Avenue. Deeper pools are formed by rocky outcroppings here. Some provide good holding water and nearly always have fish when they are running in this section of the river. Access is down a steep bluff as far downstream as the new freeway bridge. Many side roads take off from the old highway.

Pepperwood

There is an access point at the upstream end of the town of Pepperwood at the city limit sign on the old highway. This area, too, features slow, deep holes worth fishing.

There is a summer, low-water bridge at Shively. This provides total access as far downstream as Holms and Holms Bar. Some of the deepest holding water in this section of the river is formed by steep bluffs nearby. There is another bridge at the upstream end of Holms Bar that provides access.

High Rock

Probably the surest spot to find steelies in this area is at High Rock. A very deep hole, which even in summer is thirty feet or more, has formed at the rock. Steelheads pause in this area on their upstream migration. They lie in this hole while waiting for the water to rise.

There is an access road through the redwoods and Founders Grove just past where the old highway crosses the South Fork of the Eel. This roads leads to a sand and gravel operation and a good group of riffles with some shallow holes. This is not holding water, but it is good because the stream is pinched together here and forms deep riffles. Access is down a steep bluff or through the gravel operation. At low water you can fish this area by wading the shallows above the riffles.

At McCann, a railroad siding, there is a bridge to the east side. A series of extremely long pools is formed here. These deep holes normally hold fish, but they are difficult to fish because they are so big.

Access is very limited along the main Eel. The areas at Eel Rock and Cain Rock are generally the best sections of the main Eel. If the angler doesn't have specific information that a run of fish is in the river in this area, it hardly pays to make the long side trip. After the first storms of the season, the angler will probably do better fishing the South Fork because access points are so much better.

South Fork Eel River

Access is nearly total along the entire stretch of the South Fork because the highway closely follows the river. The access points are obvious to any angler traveling Highway 101 in this section. No single area is better than another except immediately above and below Benbow Dam. The best way to fish the river here is to float it in a rubber raft. Using a raft, you can reach every section of the stream.

Middle Fork Eel River

Access is the biggest problem in fishing the Middle Fork. Except for a short stretch where the Covelo Road crosses the river, and another stretch near the canyon off the Covelo–Corning Road, the river runs through private property. The section of canyon on the Middle Fork near the ranger station is noted for summer steelhead fishing. In the winter steelheads generally do not hold in the valley section below the canyon mouth but in the steep canyon where deep holes are. Best access, even here, is at the bridge on the Corning Road. Above this point the river is nearly inaccessible.

Spy Rock, Dos Rios, Van Arsdale

The upper section of the Eel River at Van Arsdale Dam can be important to the late-season fisherman. There are many spawning sections in the upper river and steelies tend to hold in these canyons far better than they do further downstream in the river. Access is by means of the few roads indicated on the map of this section.

Generally, the upper river is made up of deep holding pools and short riffles of average depth. The best places to fish, due to the limited access, are the areas near feeder streams. Steelies will hold in the pools near the mouths of the feeder creeks waiting for the water to rise so they can move into them to spawn. At one time this upper section of the river was a prime holding and fishing area, but extensive lumbering in the drainage above this area has caused a serious silting problem and a drop in the productivity of the entire upper river.

The river directly below Van Arsdale Dam is a special spot. All steelies heading upstream eventually end up between the dam and Tomki and Thomas Creeks. Heavy rains are needed to bring the water level up in this area. It is generally not a good spot until after the first of the year. River flow is controlled by releases from the large dam at Lake Pillsbury. This means winter flows can be moderate in the Van Arsdale section even if it is a very wet season.

Access is limited in the upper river to only a few miles of stream, but some of the best fishing in the entire Eel River drainage can be found below Van Arsdale Dam. Rough roads follow both sides of the river for a short distance downstream from the egg-taking station at Van Arsdale Dam. In general, steelies hit best here in the holes. They are more restless than fish

taken in downstream areas and can be seen jumping nearly all the time. The riffles are mostly very short between the holes and not very suitable for fly fishing. This section of the river is reached through Potter Valley off Highway 20 between Ukiah and Clear Lake.

Van Duzen River

The Van Duzen, tributary to the Eel River, is a fine steelhead stream in its own right. Access is the key to good fishing and the Van Duzen, in its important stretches, is accessible.

Highway 101 Bridge

The best access point to the lower river on the Van Duzen is located just at the north end of the Highway 101 Bridge that spans the river near its junction with the Eel River. This road leads down to the bar near the bridge and connects with an extensive road system along the bar. These roads are often rough and care should be used when taking a passenger car on them.

Under the bridge, along the south edge of the river and a bit upstream, is the first of what I call the Chalk Bluff Pools. These are unique in that they form deep pools wherever they are located. Any steelies in the river will hole up to rest in these deep pools. The bulk of the water in the Van Duzen is shallow most of the year. The river wanders along its streambed and forms shallow pools connected with shallow riffles. Steelheads have to pass through these areas but normally they will not hold in shallows. This makes the few deeper sections like the Chalk Bluff Holes very important.

A pickup camper is ideal for working the coast streams. At the Van Duzen the angler should keep on the move, fishing many different spots until a concentration of fish is found.

Fisher Road

The next access point to the Van Duzen is Fisher Road. This road takes off from Highway 36 on a bluff just to the west of the small town of Carlotta. The road leads down the bluff to the river. This is a good fly fishing area at low-water stages and a good drift fishing spot at higher water stages. There is a low-water bridge on Fisher Road. These low-water bridges are spotted along the river either for access to south bank lumbering operations or to ranches that cannot be reached directly by regular roads. These bridges normally wash out during high water.

Chalk Bluff Pools

The main Chalk Bluff Pools on the Van Duzen can be reached by watching for highway paddle board No. 12.85. These highway markers are posted on all roads. The access road system leads to a series of very deep chalk holes that will always have steelheads in them when the fish are in the river. You can spot the holes by watching for the distinctive chalk bluff that comes down into the water. The pools form at the base of these cliffs. These are excellent fly, lure, or bait pools at all times.

Bridges

There are two bridges at each end of a big bar where the river loops to the north. There are some good, deep holes at the lower bridge and some good fly fishing pools around the edge of the bar. Access is through

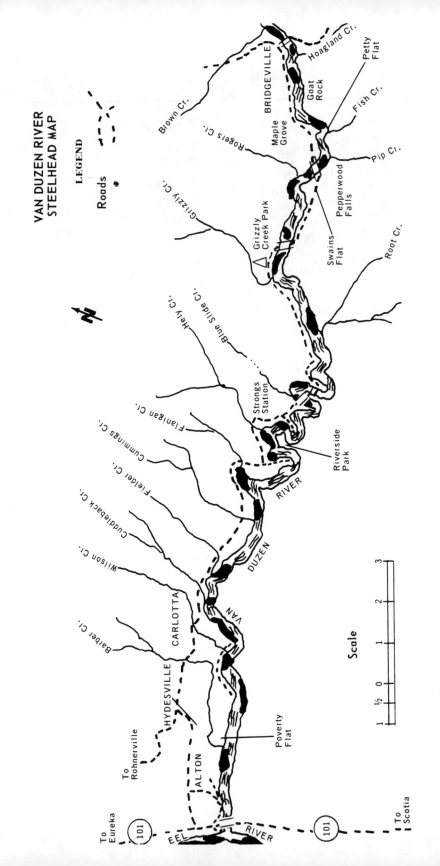

VAN DUZEN RIVER
STEELHEAD MAP

LEGEND

Roads

Scale

1 ½ 0 1 2 3

road systems in a redwood grove.

At the upper bridge there is a good access road that takes off just at the north end of the bridge to the river on the river side. This road leads to the top end of the Chalk Bluff area and has some excellent, deep pools.

One and a half miles upstream there is another lumber access road to the river in a short valley. Most of this water is shallow pools and riffles. This is fair for fly fishing when the water is at medium depths.

West Park

Two miles upstream from the upper bridge is an access point at the west end of Grizzly Creek State Park. This area is better than most on the upper Van Duzen because it features rocks and deep holding pools. Access is down the steep shore to the rock and rubble section of stream that can be seen from the rest area here.

The access in the camping area of the park is to relatively shallow pools. This area should only be fished after the first good storms.

Bridge Access

There is an access point to some good fly and baitfishing water at a bridge two miles above the state park. This access area stretches for nearly a mile downstream from the bridge and is reached directly from the highway.

There is a single access point to more fly and bait water 3.5 miles upstream from the bridge. This single access point to this section of stream is through an abandoned lumber mill readily seen from the highway. Gravel operations here have gouged out deeper spots that hold steelies.

Bridge Access

Another bridge provides access to another shallow, riffle section of the river a mile above the abandoned mill. This area marks the beginning of a steep canyon area.

Goat Rock

The Goat Rock area is one of the best on the entire Van Duzen. Goat Rock is a huge rock outcropping on the south side of the river. Through the years huge chunks of rock have broken off and remain in the stream bed. As the river flows over these rocks, it forms very deep holding pools that steelheads utilize at low-water periods. If there are any steelies in this section of the river, they will be found in these holes. Access is by steep trail just downstream from Goat Rock on the north shore. A large turnout provides ample parking for anglers here.

Bridgeville

Between Goat Rock and Bridgeville, the upper limit of legal winter fishing, there is a deep canyon. It is a distance of a little less than 2.5 miles between these two landmarks. Most of the canyon is not accessible to the angler. There is one direct access point 1.2 miles above Goat Rock. This entire area is a good holding area because much of the stream bed is formed by huge rocks interspersed with gravel to make it ideal.

The last access point is in Bridgeville down the banks near the store. This whole area has deep holes that are holding areas, especially during the low-water periods of the season. Steelies tend to lay over in these holes waiting for fresh storms to raise the water level in the upper river so that they can go upstream to spawn.

Mattole River

The Mattole River is little known by California steelhead fishermen. Most of the lack of knowledge is because this stream is off the beaten path. It is a very fine river, however. There are about twenty-nine miles of good fishing from the mouth to the upstream limit of legal fishing at Honeydew Creek.

The thing that makes the Mattole so outstanding is that more than 100 inches of rain falls in this drainage each year. This compares with perhaps thirty or forty inches of rain in other nearby streams. Even in very dry years, the Mattole usually gets at least twice as much rain as other streams in this area. This can be important in years when rain does not move the fish into other streams.

The Department of Fish and Game has made it illegal to fish at the mouth of the Mattole. When the sandbar goes out at the mouth and steelies enter the stream, they are too easy to catch. The first good spots for steelheading are down the sandbar about a quarter-mile from the mouth. A good road on the south bank services all areas down to the lagoon at the mouth of the river. Best holding spots are at the high-tide mark against the north bluff.

There are roads down to the river bar every mile or so along the length of the road upstream from the mouth. In dry years steelies will move into the first few miles of river and hole up in wide, fairly shallow holes. At these times you can see them finning restlessly in the pools if you use polaroid glasses. They are very spooky in the clear water and you have to wait until a breeze ruffles the water before you cast even a lightly rigged fly over them.

The area between tidewater and the Petrolia Bridge is dotted with good holes. In general, the riffles offer pretty poor fishing until there is a substantial rain in the drainage. Some of the best fishing in the Mattole can be found in the area below Petrolia, especially in late fall and early winter.

Petrolia

The best access in the Petrolia area is along the Conklin Creek Road that runs on the north bank. The most notable spot is the deep hole at the base of the U.S.G.S. gauging station on this road. The steelies pause in this deep hole to rest before moving further upstream.

At Conklin Creek there is a huge hole just below where it enters the Mattole. This area is good just about any time of the season.

South Bank Road

There is an access point one mile upstream from the Petrolia Bridge on the South Bank Road. There are also some good holes at the bridge.

For the next two miles upstream, the river bed features rocks running from the size of a hat to the size of a bushel basket. This area is excellent for steelies, especially after a modest rain because fish can always find spots to rest out of the current. Some deep pockets have been dredged out where the current rushes against the rocky shoreline.

Bridges

About five miles above the Petrolia

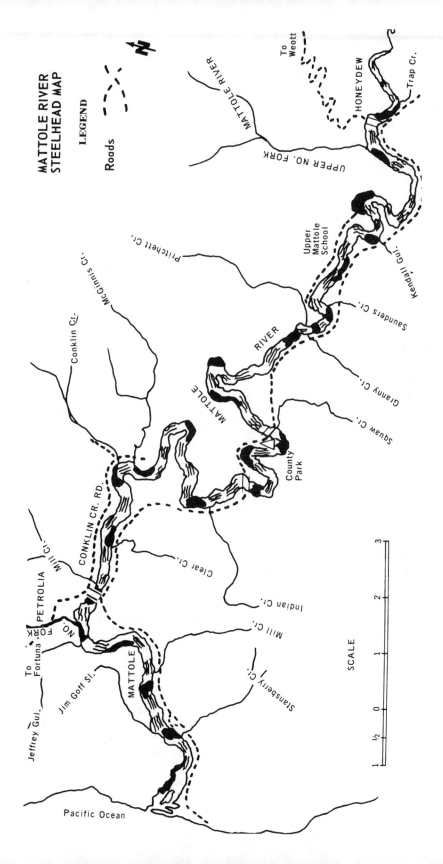

MATTOLE RIVER
STEELHEAD MAP

LEGEND

Roads

N

SCALE

1   ½   0   1   2   3

Pacific Ocean

Jeffrey Gul.

To Fortuna

PETROLIA

NO. FORK

Mill Cr.

Jim Goff Sl.

MATTOLE

CONKLIN CR. RD.

Conklin Cr.

McGinnis Cr.

Pritchett Cr.

Clear Cr.

Indian Cr.

Mill Cr.

Stansberry Cr.

County Park

MATTOLE

RIVER

Squaw Cr.

Granny Cr.

Saunders Cr.

Kendall Gul.

Upper Mattole School

UPPER NO. FORK

MATTOLE RIVER

To Weott

HONEYDEW

Trap Cr.

Bridge, there are two other bridges that offer direct access to the river from either the county park or along rough roads beside the bars. This area is particularly productive because it has a good combination of deep pools and rock formations. Steelies can rest either in the larger and deeper pools or in the tiny pools at the rocky formations. This is a good bait and lure area, but fly fishermen of even modest casting ability can also score.

Access is difficult for the next few miles above the county park bridge, but the river has some fine deep holes that are worth the effort. Some of the best holding water in the Mattole can be found here.

Lindley Road

At Lindley Road there is a bridge across the river to the north side. This road provides access to a stretch that features willow-lined banks. A good rain is needed before steelies will be in this area. Fish under the cut-banks and where the willows overhang and sweep the current.

Honeydew

There is good access in the Honeydew area, but the area downstream to Lindley Road is frequently posted. There is some direct access two miles below Honeydew and anglers can enter the streambed here to work the river. There are quite a few deep holes, but mostly the river is fine gravel and sand, not very good holding water.

Tenmile River

Access to the water is the main problem facing anglers wanting to fish the Tenmile River. The lower river is reached off a road running a short distance upstream in the tidal basin at the north end of the Highway 1 bridge. Launching is not currently possible here.

Lumber company roads service the entire Tenmile drainage, but use of these roads is severely restricted the year around. These are private roads and permission, as well as current information should be sought before using these roads. Primary access point is in Fort Bragg where the road ends in the Boise Cascade Union Lumber Company Yard.

Noyo River

The Noyo River is the main stream in this section of the Mendocino Coast fishery. Access at the mouth of the river for small boat launching is located on the north and south sides of the river. The ramp on the south side is reached a short distance off Highway 1 from Highway 20.

Fishing tidewater is a good bet in the Noyo. Steelies generally arrive early in this stream and hold in the tidal section below the railroad bridge until the first rains. They are on hand here for longer periods than they are in most of the coastal streams. You can use a small boat to fish the many deep holes in the lower Noyo and to reach the area above Newman Gulch. After a light rain, the area just above tidewater is excellent fishing.

Angling access to most of the Noyo River can be gained by utilizing the Skunk (California Western) Railroad, which travels the entire Noyo Canyon. The railroad will pick up and drop off anglers at any spot

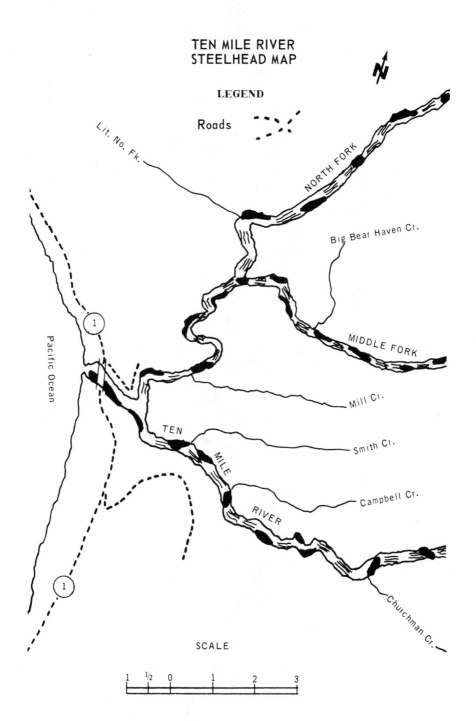

TEN MILE RIVER
STEELHEAD MAP

LEGEND

Roads

Lit. No. Fk.

NORTH FORK

Big Bear Haven Cr.

MIDDLE FORK

Mill Cr.

Pacific Ocean

TEN

Smith Cr.

MILE

Campbell Cr.

RIVER

Churchman Cr.

SCALE

1 ½ 0 1 2 3

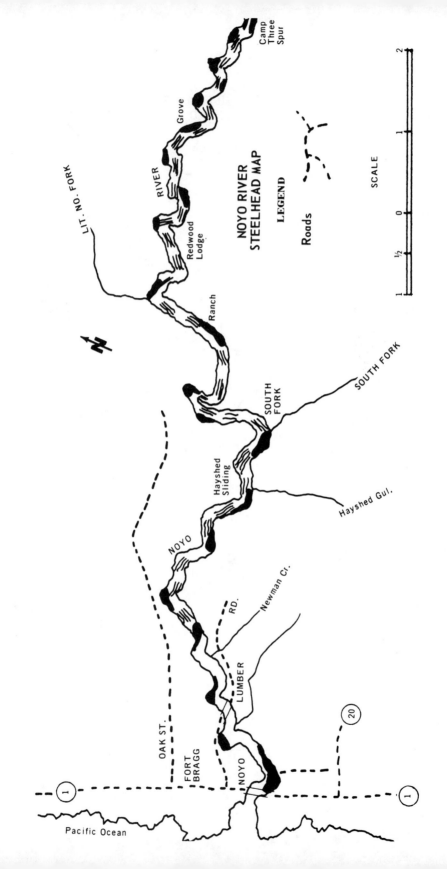

NOYO RIVER
STEELHEAD MAP

LEGEND

Roads

SCALE

along the river. The best spots to be dropped off are near the major tributaries such as Hayshed Gulch, Little North Fork, South Fork, and the upper limit of legal fishing near Camp Three Spur.

Other good spots with good pools and riffles will be found at Redwood Lodge and Grove. The crew will drop you at the right spots if you tell them where you want to fish.

Big River

Big River is a wide, deep river in its entire lower section. It is virtually one long series of deep holes with few, if any, riffles at any stage of water flow. Most anglers launch at the mouth on the north shore and fish the river up as far as Big River Laguna from a boat. Trolling, still fishing, and casting when surfacing fish are sighted are all good methods.

There are many pilings and snags in this part of Big River. Steelies hold in areas like this because the current during winter runoff has gouged out deep holes and pockets. When the water is roiled, it is difficult to spot the many huge logs and snags. Boating anglers should be careful because many large bars jut out into the water.

The lumber companies have roads along Big River, but they usually close them to auto traffic. Anglers may walk these roads to reach all sections of the stream. In cases where these roads are closed, there is usually a reason. Get information on current conditions at the Fort Bragg office of Boise Cascade Company.

Big Laguna Creek

The river is running above Big La-

guna Creek and anglers would do well to fish this area. Steelies hold in the area just above and just below the still water section before heading further upstream. These spots are prime fishing areas. The first few miles of the river above a low-water bridge at the mouth of Big Laguna Creek are the best spots.

Mendocino Woodlands

There is an access point to the upper part of Big River at Mendocino Woodlands. To reach this section take either the Graveyard Road at Caspar off Highway 1 or the Little Lake Road off Highway 1 at Mendocino.

This section has several good riffles and deep holes. This is a state forest recreation area. This part of the river, from here to Two Log Creek, the upstream limit of legal fishing, only has fish after the first heavy storms of winter or fall.

Albion River

Access to the Albion River is very limited due to heavy posting by landowners and because there just are not that many streamside roads.

Lower River

All of the lower river, in the tidewater sections at least, is open to boat fishermen. You can launch and fish the deep holes scattered throughout the tidal stretch at the fishing village at Albion Flat at the north end of the Highway 1 bridge. A road runs along the north side of the river from this resort.

Upper Albion

The upper limit of legal fishing is at

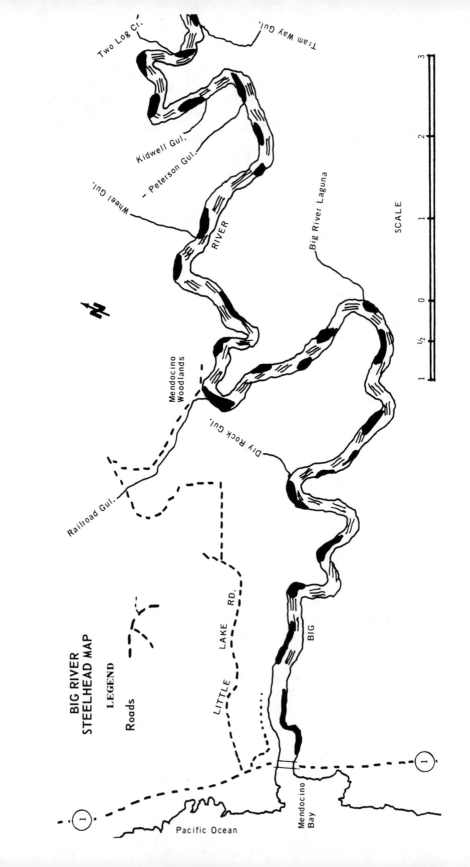

BIG RIVER
STEELHEAD MAP

LEGEND

Roads

SCALE

3 2 1 0 ½ 1

Two Log Cr.

Tram Way Gul.

Kidwell Gul.

Peterson Gul.

Wheel Gul.

RIVER

Big River Laguna

Mendocino
Woodlands

Dry Rock Gul.

Railroad Gul.

LITTLE LAKE RD.

BIG

Pacific Ocean

Mendocino Bay

1

1

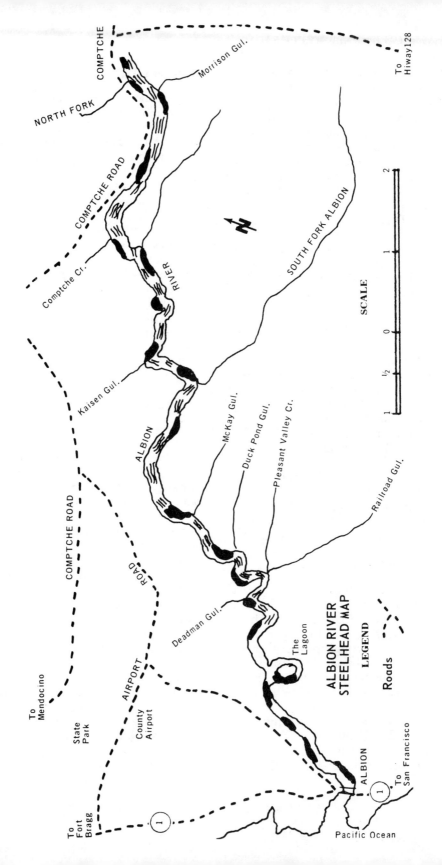

ALBION RIVER
STEELHEAD MAP

LEGEND

Roads ---

SCALE

1 ½ 0 1 2

To Hiway128

COMPTCHE

NORTH FORK

Morrison Gul.

COMPTCHE ROAD

Comptche Cr.

RIVER

SOUTH FORK ALBION

Kaisen Gul.

ALBION

McKay Gul.

Duck Pond Gul.

Pleasant Valley Cr.

Railroad Gul.

COMPTCHE ROAD

AIRPORT ROAD

ROAD

To
Mendocino

State
Park

County Airport

Deadman Gul.

The Lagoon

ALBION

To
San Francisco

1

To
Fort Bragg

1

Pacific Ocean

the North Fork of the Albion. The last few miles are directly accessible to the fisherman from the Comptche Road, which runs along the stream in this area. The North Fork is not marked on the highway, but it is crossed by the only good-sized bridge on this road. The North Fork enters within a mile or so of the small town of Comptche.

This section of the river must be fished with bait because the river is very narrow and casting is out of the question in most areas. The area at the North Fork always has many fish when they are running.

Navarro River

The Navarro River is one of the longer and more extensive streams in the Mendocino–Sonoma Loop system of steelhead waters. It carries a good head of water the year around in most of its major tributaries. This means the survival rate among fish in this stream is a bit higher than in most others. The extensive fishery is limited only by the access available. The Navarro has fairly good access when compared to some of the other streams.

Lower Navarro

The first access point to the lower river is located at the south end of the Highway 1 Bridge. A road heads toward the bar at the south end of the river through property owned by Navarro-by-the-Sea resort. This road ends on the south bar and anglers can fish here and in the lower lagoon.

The road that heads upstream from the Highway 1 bridge on the south side is private and permission must be sought to fish from this road.

Highway 128

Access is nearly total along the north shore from Highway 128 to the mouth of the North Fork at Dimmick State Park. There are numerous turnouts on the highway where an angler can park and walk down to the water's edge. There are several spots set aside by the Redwood Industries Association for angling access. In some of these groves, there are good rough campsites.

One of the key spots for steelhead fishing in this section is at and near Dimmick State Park. The North Fork enters here and is one of the major tributaries of the river. Steelies hold in the many pools in this area waiting to migrate up the North Fork, which is closed to fishing.

Upstream Access

There are many road systems that skirt the Navarro River upstream and down from the mouth of the North Fork, but these are nearly all either chained off or posted against public use by the Masonite Company. If they were open to cars, the fisherman could have almost total access. However, these roads can be used for walking and anglers willing to do a lot of this are able to fish a great deal of stream.

County Road 132 or the Greenwood Ridge Road crosses the Navarro at Hendy State Park and is an access point to the river at the extreme upper limit of legal fishing. There are many good runs of water reached by a trail leading to the water from the south end of the bridge. There are good holes all along the Navarro where you find large rocks in the stream or where the shoreline is formed by rocks.

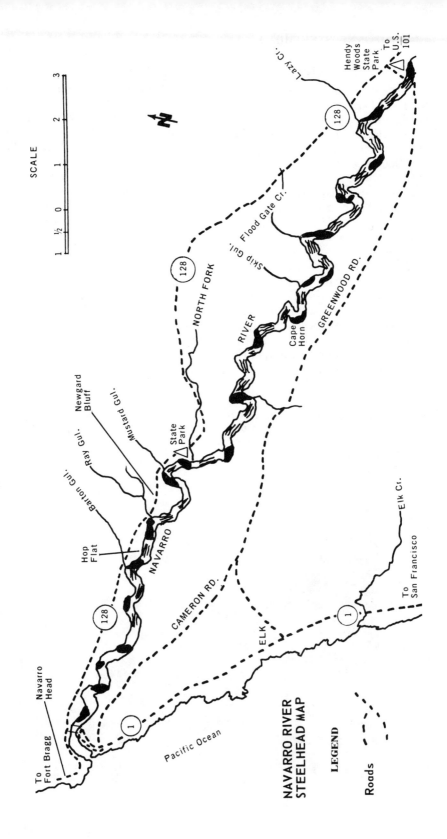

NAVARRO RIVER
STEELHEAD MAP

LEGEND

Roads

Garcia River

The lower Garcia River is noted for the big runs of large fish after the first few rainstorms of the year. This part of the river normally is best from December through the end of the season. The section where tides affect the river, usually to a point just above Minor Hole, is the most productive part of the stream until big storms arrive and the fish head upstream.

An access road provided by the county heads toward the tidal basin of the Garcia along the south shore. To locate this road, look for a cliff that runs out to Point Arena Lighthouse. The road is located at the base of this cliff and ends at a parking area near the lower river.

The best bet for fishing the lower river is to ford the stream at the parking area and fish from the north side. This will allow access to the holes and tidal basin down to the mouth of the river. When steelies are entering the river, you can often see them working their way over shallow bars in the tidal basin. They hole up in the big pool at Minor Hole until heavy rains raise the river.

Highway 1 Bridge

There is an access point at Highway 1 Bridge. A long series of shallow riffles and fairly deep holes is located downstream. Upstream from the bridge, most of the stream consists of relatively shallow holes and rough riffles.

The famous Minor Hole on the Garcia River is located at the base of the large knoll at the left. Anglers line this area at the upper edge of tide movement. Each tide brings more fish into the river and they pause here.

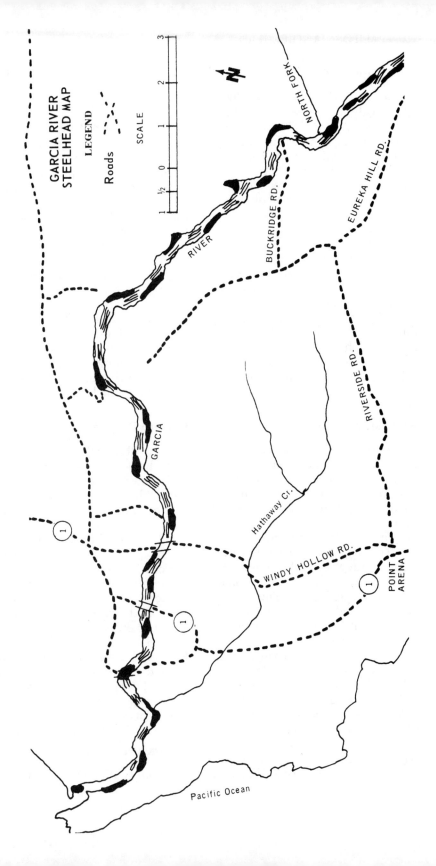

Boonville Road

There is an access point off Boonville Road a few miles from where the road heads east. There are several good holes and good riffles for fly, lure, and bait fishing. This is an excellent baitfishing section. The road is the first well-paved road that heads south to the river off Boonville Road.

Just at the point where the Boonville road leaves Highway 1, there is another road off the highway. This is Windy Hollow Road, which ends at the town of Point Arena. The road crosses a shallow-water bridge that provides crossing during the summer. This access point has shallow pools and riffles that are ideal for fly fishing and bait drifting. A gravel operation here has made some bar access roads.

Riverside Road

Riverside Road heads east from Highway 1 in the town of Point Arena and two access roads of importance can be taken from this road. Also, Windy Hollow Road heads north from this road in the city limits of Point Arena.

The first access road is Buckridge Road. This road is unmarked, but it can be recognized by the signs for Buckridge Ranch. The road is steep and ends up at a series of fly and bait riffles that are among the finest in the river.

The second access road, Eureka Hill Road, also is unmarked. Just follow the signs for County Road 505. The bridge on this road provides access to the upper stretches of legal fishing. It is not legal to fish above the bridge. Access is somewhat restricted by private property in this area. There are good bait and lure holes and some fair fly riffles here.

Gualala River

The tidewater section of the Gualala River is probably more fished and more important to visiting anglers than any other part of the stream. The main access point to the lower river and the area near the mouth is at the north end of the Highway 1 bridge.

The access point allows anglers to drive a road system along the gravel bar at the mouth on the north bank. The south bank is made up almost entirely of high cliffs. The pools near the mouth against the south bank are among the most productive in the rivers in this area. Small boats can be launched.

County Road Access

County Road 501 runs along the north bank of the Gualala and starts off Highway 1 a short distance from the bridge. This is a surfaced, all-weather highway. A short distance along this road, it joins County Road 502. At this point there is an old road that has been abandoned: the old Highway 1. An angler can park and walk down to the upper stretches of tidewater from this point and from a big field at the local cemetery.

About a mile from Highway 1 is Redwood Park, a private campground where access for guests is available. There are several large pools that hold steelies when they are in this part of the stream.

Upstream Access

The county road ends at the North

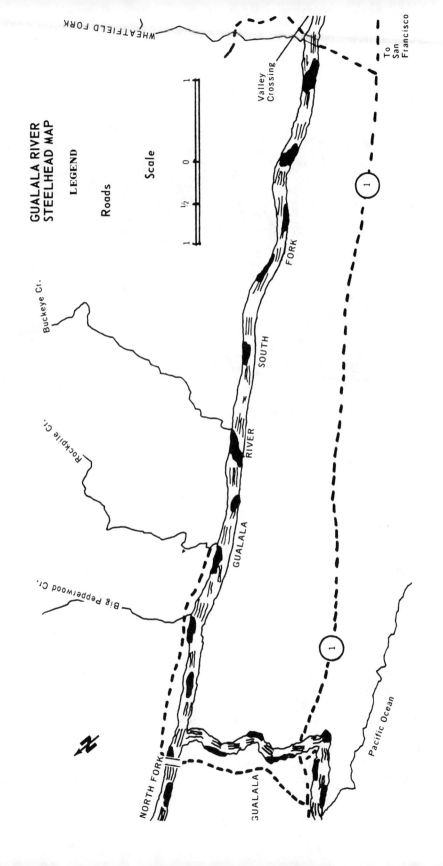

GUALALA RIVER
STEELHEAD MAP

LEGEND

Roads

Scale

WHEATFIELD FORK

Valley
Crossing

To San
Francisco

SOUTH   FORK

GUALALA   RIVER

Buckeye Cr.

Rockpile Cr.

Big Pepperwood Cr.

NORTH FORK

GUALALA

Pacific Ocean

In order to get down deep enough to take winter-run steelies, it is often necessary to cast directly upstream and draw the fly back toward the rod. This method allows maximum depth for the fly caster.

Fork and there is restricted access along the road, much of it through private property. Along the east side of the South Fork, there is an excellent lumber company road. This road is posted and permission must be obtained before using it. There are many short roads leading to the better sections of the river from this road.

At the Sea Ranch development, there is an access point off the Valley Crossing Road, marked Annapolis at the highway, to the upper stretches of legal fishing. A road system on the bars here through a gravel operation provides access. The best bet is to work along the east bank because the Sea Ranch developers have posted a forty-acre section of land on the west bank for their own people. There are some good holes in this area.

Russian River

Most of the steelhead fishing in the lowest section of the Russian River is done either from the two sandbars at the mouth or from a boat in the tidal lagoon.

Access to the north and south bars at the mouth is good. On the south side access is through Goat Rock State Beach. There are large parking areas and it is a short trip across the sandbar to the mouth of the river.

Access to the north bar is either

down the cliff from Highway 1 where the road turns away from the river or from one of the numerous pullouts in this section where a car can be parked. There are several trails down to the beach in this area.

Another access point is at River's End Cafe. Here, for a fee, you can launch a small boat, camp, and fish either the lagoon or the north bar at the mouth of the river.

To Highway 1 Bridge

The access points for bank fishing are numerous along Highway 1 between the mouth and just upstream from the small town of Jenner. There is a single rough launching site in this stretch of highway. There is considerable private, posted property in this stretch.

The water in this section is made up of several deep holes. From the bank bait and lure fishing is the best bet. Many anglers fish with flies, lures, and bait in this area. Fly fishing is possible but limited normally to anglers fishing from a boat.

At the south end of the Highway 1 bridge there is a trailer park and launch area. Upstream on the south bank access is limited to Willow Creek, where the road turns away from the stream.

Highway 116 Access

Highway 116 starts at the north end of the Highway 1 bridge and heads upstream on the north bank. This area is noted for many fine holding pools. It can be fished from the bank in some spots between the bridge and the Duncan Mills Bridge, but boat fishing the area is easier.

For a fee you can launch a boat at Foresti's to fish this stretch. Trolling or bait and lure casting is good in this area below Duncan Mills Bridge. The tidal movements have a great effect on fish in this section of stream. The flood and ebb tides are the best times to fish, or just when the tides reverse the flow.

Duncan Mills

There are good access points to deep pools and riffles near Duncan Mills Bridge. Access is at both ends of the bridge. Freezeout Road heads downstream from the south end of the bridge for a short distance. One mile down this road is an access road to the beaches, pools, and riffles in this section. You can fish either from a boat at high tide or by wading. This is an excellent stretch of fly and drift water.

Moscow Road

Moscow Road heads upriver on the south bank. The best access point is at the Casini Ranch. You can fish and camp for a fee at the famous Brown's Pool area. This also allows access to the Austin Riffle section, one of the most productive spots on the lower river. The riffle is named for the creek.

Above Casini's the river is nearly one solid, deep pool between Austin Riffle and the town of Monte Rio. Except for a single spot for shore fishing, along Moscow Road at Villa Grande, most of this pool, Moscow Pool, is best fished from a boat. You can launch a boat either at the head of Austin Riffle or from a public launch at Monte Rio Bridge. There is good access at both ends of the bridge.

On the Highway 116, or north, side of the river, there are several direct access points at turnouts.

These anglers have zeroed in on the holding section of Brown's Pool on the Russian. Working from a small skiff is often better than wading because it gives you control over the position from which to approach the holds.

There is also access at Austin Creek and just below where the creek enters the river to the big rock that forms the north side of Brown's Pool. There is a lot of private, posted property in this stretch and only a few spots are open to the public.

Monte Rio

All the access on the south, or west bank, is through private property above Monte Rio. Access on the north, or east side, is direct from the highway in this section. There are several good pools here, but few can be reached directly from the highway.

There is a good series of pools at Northwood. These are difficult to find, but they are worth the effort. There are two summer bridges between Northwood and the Guerne-ville Bridge on Highway 12. The bridges get washed out, or at least are made unusable, after the first heavy rains of the season. They are good access points.

The lower bridge is at Odd Fellows Road, just upstream from the Korbel winery vineyards. The other is at Guernewood Road from both sides of the river. There is good access at the Highway 12 bridge just above Guerneville, at the east end of the bridge.

Rio Nido and Rio Dell

The area above Guerneville has restricted access between the city and Mirabel Park. There are access points along the highway and at the bridge at Hacienda. There are a few, limited access points off the Old River Road at the south end of the

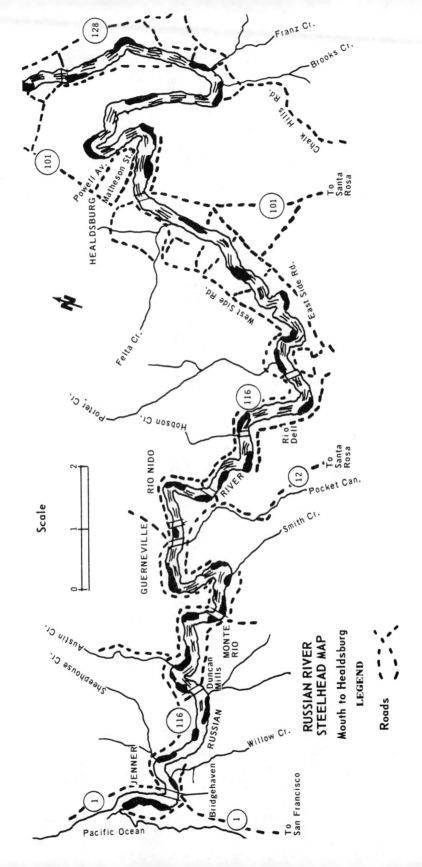

RUSSIAN RIVER
STEELHEAD MAP
Mouth to Healdsburg

LEGEND

Roads

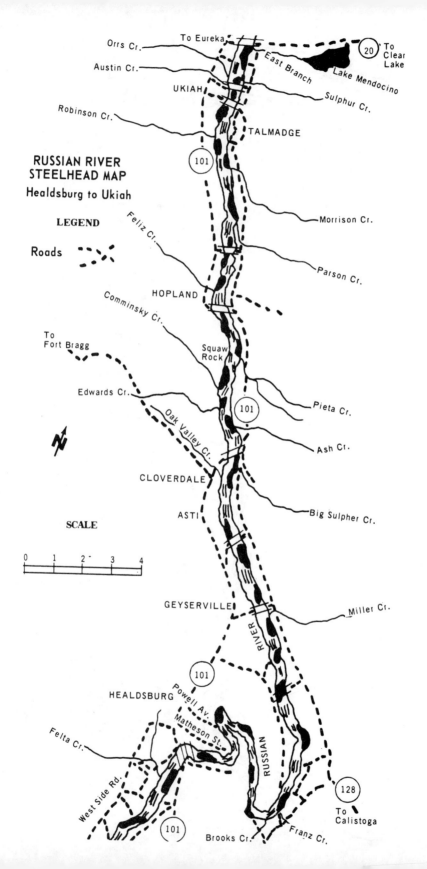

bridge at Hacienda. This road is reached by taking the Forest Hills Road at the south end of the bridge. A great deal of private property is posted and the best access is down the bars from the few spots where a visiting angler can get to the water.

Mirabel Park has some excellent pools and riffles. There is a fee for access here. Access on the Highway 116 side or West Bank Road is restricted except for a mile or so above the Hacienda Bridge and a half-mile above the Wohler Bridge. At Wohler Bridge there are some excellent riffles and pools. Access is at the bridge.

The East Bank Road above Mirabel Park has little access except through private property of the vineyard and orchard owners between the Wohler Bridge and Healdsburg. If you get permission, be sure to ask if the landowner will allow you to drive to the river. These roads are very soft and after any kind of rain they will be ruined by driving them.

Basalt Rock Company

On the outskirts of Healdsburg, the Basalt Rock Company is an access point on the old River Highway. Very heavy trucks operate here along a levee road, but there are several places where an angler can pull off so as not to block traffic. This road heads under the new Freeway Bridge on Highway 101. West bank access is down the freeway off-ramp north of this point.

Healdsburg to Cloverdale

Access in Healdsburg is good from the bridges in town. Several good holding pools and riffle waters can be found right in town and along the river on the huge bend in the Russ-

ian. There are many good fly fishing areas here where long casts are not needed. From Healdsburg to Cloverdale most of the access is from the bridges that cross the river.

Beyond Cloverdale, where Highway 101 crosses the river and recrosses it above Squaw Rock, most of the access is directly from the highway and its many pullouts. Stretches of white water and short riffles interspersed with deep pools provide excellent fishing. This stretch is one of the most popular for visiting anglers because of its easy access. This is a good area for late season fishing. Of particular note are the deep holes at and below Squaw Rock.

Above Hopland

The only real access for the general public above Hopland is at the many bridges that cross the river. The orchards and vineyards in this area have very soft ground and vehicle traffic must be limited to prevent rutting. If the water level is running at normal depths, access can be gained to nearly all this part of the river by walking the sand and gravel bars. It is necessary to wade frequently because the river winds from one bank to the other.

This area of the Russian is particularly good late in the season. The water is usually dirty here, due to releases from the dam at Lake Mendocino. Often on the weekends dam releases are reduced to help clear the water.

It is not necessary to have long distance tackle in these upper stretches of the Russian. The river, when it is at fishable levels, is a fairly small stream. When any amount of heavy rain falls, the upper river rises quickly due to the fact that the soil is loose from extensive agricultural use.

San Lorenzo River

The San Lorenzo River is included as the only stream south of the Golden Gate in this guide because it is most typical of the streams that enter the Pacific in this area. The San Lorenzo is a small, short stream. It carries a good head of water during the winter months and steelies crowd into it after the first heavy rains, usually from December on.

The San Lorenzo is the best of the southern streams that have steelhead runs. It is the most consistent producer. The other small creeks in this area are best fished by local residents rather than by visitors who have a limited amount of time.

Most of the fishing done in the San Lorenzo River by visiting anglers is done in the lower few miles in the city of Santa Cruz. This is a perfect area for the fly fisherman and for the angler who has mastered the art of drift fishing with light and sensitive gear. Access is better for the visitor in this section than in most parts of the river.

Special regulations apply to these streams south of the Golden Gate. You can fish on opening and closing days, Wednesday, Saturday and Sunday, and on legal holidays. You can only keep two steelhead or two steelhead and salmon in combination. The upper limit of legal fishing is the Lomond Bridge in Boulder Creek.

San Lorenzo Access

In the lower river near the tidal section of the stream, there are several bridges and an extensive levee system where the river passes through Santa Cruz.

As a general rule, the area from the mouth to the small dam is sandy bottom with few holes of any consequence. The flood control people even have placed signs on the levee system asking that rocks not be thrown into the stream. Rocks will cause the stream to dig holes and disturb the even flow of the river through the city.

Just about all of the river from the city limits of Santa Cruz to Boulder Creek is brush lined. At fairly low water you can wade virtually down the middle of the river. The steelies hold along and under the sweepers of brush and foliage and rarely will be found in the open, moving water. When the water is clear, you can make quartering and downstream casts to get a bait, lure, or fly near the sweepers.

The best access to the middle part of the river is through Henry Cowell State Park. The park has an extensive trail system. There are also access points at Old Ox Road and Rincon Service Road.

The best way to fish the upper sections of the stream is to gain access either through the park or through the spots where the road crosses the river and float down the stream in an inner tube when the water is running at a high level. With one of these tubes and a pair of chest or armpit waders, you can float down the current and fish virtually all of the water in the stream effectively.

Railroad Bridge Hole

One hole of consequence is located just above the railroad bridge near the mouth of the river. The hole is along the sharp cliff on the south bank and can be reached readily with a fairly short cast. Steelies hold here to rest after battling their

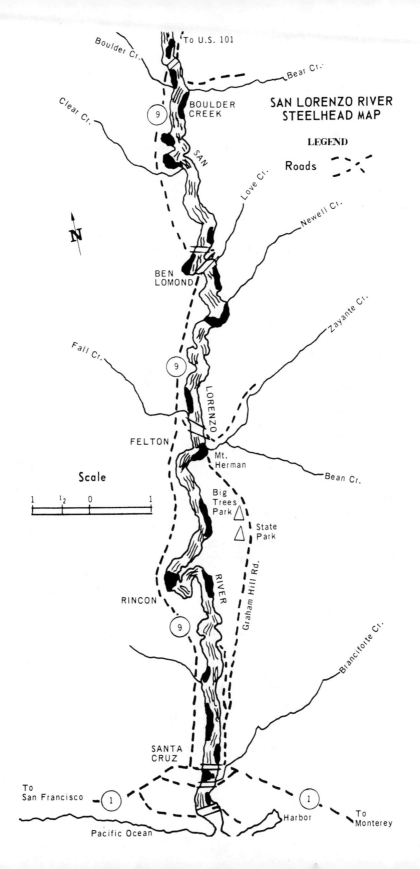

way across the sandbar at the mouth. The rest of this section features shallow, sandy bottom and steelies move quickly through this area. Anglers line this section of the stream and try for the migrating fish as they pass by.

The Bridges

The key to fishing the lower river lies in working around the bridges. In all there are five bridges in Santa Cruz: Riverside Avenue, Laurel Street, Soquel Avenue, Water Street, and Highway 1. Steelies find their first protection from the currents near the abutments of these bridges. When the water is flowing, this is the only protection.

High Water

At very high water stages, steelheads migrate along the riprap right next to shore. At this time most anglers quit fishing, but this is one of the best times to fish with baits. Generally, the water is too roiled when it is running at a high level for lure fishing, but I have found that a Spin N Glo or other fast spinning lures will tempt steelies at this stage of the water in the San Lorenzo.

Highway 9 follows the river. About a half-mile east of Highway 1, the highway begins to climb up and away from the river. Much of this area is private property and posted. If you can gain access by permission, the best spot below the state park to fish is at Masonic Park. Another access area with good holding water and brushy shores is at the city park, Sycamore Camp Grove. Here you can park near the road and walk to the river.

Phone Ahead

If the angler is going to travel any great distance to the steelhead streams in this guide, it is best to phone ahead before making the trip, unless he's got some other source of information. The names and numbers of some sources of information are included here for convenience.

These are generally reliable business people who want to see successful fishermen. They are willing to give information on runs and weather, as long as anglers phone during business hours. I have used these people for years as my own information sources.

Smith River—Salmon Harbor, 707-487-3341; Ship A Shore, 707-487-3141
Redwood Creek—Dimmick Market, 707-488-3224, Orick
Mad River—C & L Market, 707-668-5512, Blue Lake
Salmon River—Lor-O-Ranch, 916-629-2627, Cecilville
Scott River—Rainbow Resort, 916-496-3242, Hamburg
Eel River—Darrel Brown, 707-923-2533, Garberville; Jay Grunert, Sporting Goods, 707-725-2223, Fortuna
Van Duzen River—Hydesville Market, 707-768-3604, Hydesville; Jay Grunert, Sporting Goods, 707-725-2223, Fortuna
Mattole River—Mattole Coffee Shop, 707-629-3340, Honeydew
Tenmile River—Cooney Sports, 707-964-5630, Fort Bragg
Noyo River—Sportsman Dock, 707-964-2619, Fort Bragg
Big River—Mendocino Hotel, 707-937-0511, Mendocino
Albion River—Albion Flat Fishing Village, 707-937-0606, Albion

Navarro River—Navarro Store,
  707-895-3135, Navarro
Garcia River—Disotelle's Amber
  Room, 707-882-2002, Point
  Arena
Gualala River—Gualala Hotel,
  707-884-3441, Gualala

Russian River—King's Tackle,
  707-869-2156, Guerneville
San Lorenzo River—Sportsman
  Shop, 408-423-6908, Santa
  Cruz

Appendix

I have contacted the manufacturers of the finest equipment and have compiled a sample of the suggestions of their experts.

From Martin Reel Company: Regarding salmon and steelhead equipment: In fly fishing for salmon and steelhead, we would suggest our model MG8, MG72 and 71 reels, model 3-177, 3-178, and 93-177 rods. In spin fishing, we would suggest our model 3930 and 3940 reels and 1-128 rod.

From Shakespeare: Salmon and steelhead fishing is a pretty broad and varied sport. Almost all of our tackle in one way or another can be considered appropriate for salmon and steelhead fishing.

As far as spinning tackle, all our reels in the 035 level and up are probable choices. In the casting category, all our models would be appropriate, particularly the 2900-084 with audible clicker for trolling.

Standard trolling reels we have that would be particularly effective for deep-water salmon fishing are the 2950 series reels (2950-245, 2950-350) and the 2951-355 with 5–1 gear ratio.

Fly reels that would be good

choices are the Speedex model 2802; the Beaulite reels 2812, 2814, and 2816; and the Pflueger Medalist 1494¼, 1495, 1495¼, and 1498.

All our rods in freshwater models with the exception of the ultralite would be good for salmon and steelhead fishing. We have several downrigger rods in the Ugly Stik series that are particularly effective when trolling deep for salmon.

From Quick: Tackle can vary as much as guns do in hunting. Our recommendations are:

Ocean Fishing
Rods – SRS-58, SRS-61, SRS-66, SQS-61, SQS-66
Reels – 4001, 5001, 444-XL, or conventional revolving spool reels
Line – Quick Gold Damyl 25- or 30-pound test

River Drift Fishing
Rods – CR-6M, CF-65M, QS-60, QS-65, QS-70, QS-81, SR-60, SR-65, SR-70, SR-81, PR-81
Reels – 1001, 1401, 2001, 111-XL, 121-XL, 222-XL, 022
Line – Quick Gold Damyl 12-pound test with 10-pound leader; first choice would be CF-6M with 1001 reel

Shore River Fishing
Rods – PR-81, SQS-81, SR-81
Reels – 1401, 2001, 3001, 222-XL, 022, and the new level wind 770-C and 880-C
Line – Quick Gold Damyl 12- to 15-pound test and 6- to 10-pound leader

Still Fishing from a Boat
Tackle is just about the same as for drift fishing. The big difference is in the bait – worms and hotshot lures.

From Berkeley and Company, Inc.: We manufacture equipment specifically for salmon and steelhead fishing. The items we produce aimed directly at that market are rods; our most current items are listed below along with a brief description.

BC–75 — 7½ feet — General purpose saltwater rod with Fuji ceramic casting guides, premium fiberglass featuring blank through the handle construction, chrome on brass reel seat, and double-wrapped guides

BC–91 — 8½ feet — Salmon mooching rod with the same construction features above

BC–97 — 8½RT feet — Salmon rod for wire line, has same construction features as above plus a roller tip top

BC–96 — 7½ feet — Salmon downrigger rod, same features as above, designed for downrigger fishing

BC–92 — 8 feet — Steelhead rod for casting reel with above features

BC–94 — 8 feet — Same as above, only with spinning guides

GF–92 — 9 feet — Steelhead action, featuring graphite composite construction through the handle blank and Fuji ceramic .casting guides

GF–94 — 8 feet — Same as above, except with single foot Fuji spinning guides

SG–92 — 8'2" — Steelhead action, features S-glass with graphite blank construction through the handle blank, single foot Fuji aluminum oxide casting guides, and a patented *Spinlok* handle with cork grips (great in cold and wet weather)

SG–94 — 8'2" — Same as above, only with spinning guides

In addition to rods that are specifically made for salmon and steelhead, Berkeley manufactures Trilene XL and Trilene XT, Specialist Premium Flyline, Specialist Tapered Leaders, Specialist Flyreels in three sizes, premim-quality braided Dacron, and virtually all popular lengths and sizes of fly rods.

The trade names of the specific rods I listed are as follows — all rods starting with a B are Buccaneer Series, those starting with a G are Grayfite Series, and those with an S are Shadow Series.

From Daiwa Corporation: Daiwa has an extensive array of salmon and steelhead tackle, including conventional level-wind trolling, mooching, downrigger, drift fishing, and fly fishing rods and reels.

Our Sealine 27H and 47H level-wind reels have become favored by flatline and downrigger trollers from California through the Great Lakes region. This past season we introduced the new Procaster Magforce models PMF-53H and PMF-55H, and the new Procaster Standard Series models PS-53 and PS-55 to add additional feature versatility to our salmon trolling tackle line. All six reels have a one-piece frame construction and smooth drag systems. Teamed with our new and as yet uncatalogued downrigger models in the Regal Strike series of graphite-composite rods (models 6782, 6783, 6784, 6785, and 6786), they offer potent, reliable matchups for those seeking king and silver salmon in saltwater and their freshwater counterparts, the chinooks and cohos. The same outfits make great downrigger and flatline rigs for lake trout (mackinaw) and outsized brown trout, as well.

We have an especially large selection of both conventional baitcasting and spinning rods and reels designed for the drift fishing steelheader and salmon enthusiast. Here are some especially good matchups:

Graphite Rods	Matching Daiwa Reels
PG-15	BG-16 (spinning)
PG-16	BG-16 (spinning)
PG-15C	PMF-15 (Magforce baitcasting)
PG-16C	PMF-15 (Magforce baitcasting)
PL-15	RG-1650 (rear-drag spinning)
PL-16	RG-1650 (rear-drag spinning)
PL-15C	PMF-15S (Magforce baitcasting)
PL-16C	PMF-16S (Magforce baitcasting
6715	RB-1600 (spinning)
6716	RB-1600 (spinning)
6717	RB-1600 (spinning)
6715	
6715C	PS-15 (baitcasting)
6716C	PS-15 (baitcasting)

For those who are interested in ultralight drift fishing, we make a 12-foot noodle rod, the graphite-composite Regal Strike model 6710-12.

Daiwa's Procaster Graphite Custom Series contains one of the finest steelhead fly rods you'll find anywhere. It's the model PG-47, and handles everything from an 8-weight floater to a 9-weight shooting head. The model PG-45 in this same series, which is probably the ideal Montana big trout, heavy-weighted nymph rod for a 7-weight line, also makes a super low-water, summer-run steelhead rod. It will punch out well over ninety feet with a sinking shooting head or set a dry fly down very neatly, even in windy conditions. Flyrodders who like the classic, slower action normally associated with split cane will also be pleased with our 8-weight model PG-46. It's a slow, easy-casting powerhouse that's especially pleasant when fishing a greased line for steelies. Our rim-control fly reels, models 732 and 734, match very well with all of these rods.

Daiwa offers some graphite-composite rods that are rapidly gaining reputations as all-purpose salmon and bottomfishing rods. These are our 76 and 77 actions. These are available in the Daiwa product line from high-graphite content to economical fiberglass models in the Procaster Graphite Custom, Procaster Graphite, Regal Strike, and 1300 and 1100 series. The most popular models are the PL-76 in the Procaster Graphite Series and the 6776 in the Regal Strike Series. In the fiberglass 1300 and 1100 series, the actions are those of true mooching rods. The graphite-composite and graphite versions can be used both for mooching and bottom fishing as well as for trolling with Pink Lady diving planes. They team ideally with our Sealine 27H and 47H models and with our Procaster Standard models PS-53 and PS-55.

Index

Numbers in italics refer to illustrations.